WAKING UP IS HARD TO DO

PRAISE FOR **WAKING UP IS HARD TO DO**

With wisdom, grace, humility, and tender honesty, Tom Pedulla shares his journey from altar boy to Harvard undergrad, from successful ad man to Dharma student and psychotherapist. His story, and especially the engaging way he tells it, can help us all find our way to a richer, more meaningful, more deeply connected life.——*Ronald D. Siegel, Faculty, Harvard Medical School and author of The Extraordinary Gift of Being Ordinary: Finding Happiness Right Where You Are*

In this memoir, Tom Pedulla captures ordinary moments in his unfolding life with exquisite tenderness, inviting readers to bravely explore the landscape of their own tender hearts. The transparency of his writing reflects his inner journey of self-awareness and self-acceptance. Life is mess for all of us, but in messiness there is beauty. This book proves it.——*Christopher K. Germer, Faculty, Harvard Medical School and author of The Mindful Path to Self-Compassion*

This is a book for our times. It is an elegantly written, psychologically astute, and compelling tale. Tom Pedulla takes us on a journey from the unrelenting demands in the corporate world of "Mad Men" to the freedom, wisdom and possibility in the world of "Med Men." Enjoy this unique and profound story.——*Susan M. Pollak, Co-founder of the Center for Mindfulness and Compassion at Cambridge Health Alliance and author of Self-Compassion for Parents*

Tom Pedulla's memoir is a testament to the power of the Dharma to transform the way one actually lives one's life. —— *Larry Rosenberg, Founder of Cambridge Insight Meditation Center and author of Three Steps to Awakening*

WAKING UP IS HARD TO DO

How a long lost, former altar boy found
his way home on the Buddha's Eightfold Path

THOMAS PEDULLA

WAKING UP IS HARD TO DO: How a long lost, former altar boy found his way home on the Buddha's Eightfold Path
Copyright © 2023 by Thomas Pedulla

BOOK DESIGN BY The Troy Book Makers

Printed in the United States of America

The Troy Book Makers • Troy, New York • thetroybookmakers.com

To order additional copies of this title, contact your favorite local bookstore or visit www.shoptbmbooks.com

ISBN: 978-1-61468-785-6

For Christine,
who helped me find a way

CONTENTS

AUTHOR'S NOTE

To protect their privacy, I've changed the names and other identifying details of certain people described in this book, including all the therapists who've worked with me over the years, and all the clients I worked with when I became a therapist myself.

PROLOGUE

What does it mean to wake up? To most people, it simply means opening your eyes in the morning and connecting with the world around you. It's no big deal – unless you've been in a blissful slumber and want to stay in bed instead of facing the day ahead. Then it can be a challenge.

But waking up also means paying attention, and perhaps seeing something you hadn't noticed before. Like a window that needs to be washed or a relationship that needs to be repaired. In the United States these days, many of us are waking up to the fact that despite our democratic ideals, some of our citizens continue to face discrimination, while others enjoy privileges that aren't equally available to all. This can be painful to see.

To spiritual seekers, waking up points to something that goes beyond all that, something extraordinary, elusive, and difficult to define. It's a state the Buddhists call nirvana, or enlightenment. From this place, we can see through the illusions of the material world into the true nature of reality, where the boundaries between the individual self and the rest of the universe drop away. Instead of perceiving ourselves and everything around us as separate and solid, we realize that we're all interconnected, all one, and that we – along with everyone and everything else – are constantly changing and evolving, coming and going, arising and passing away. It's a place of supreme wisdom and boundless compassion, a state of profound acceptance and peace.

I can't claim I've reached this sublime state. But I like to think I've had glimpses of it. And I've come to believe that enlightenment isn't an all-or-nothing proposition. After meditating almost every day for the past 35 years and working with some very good psychotherapists along the way, I know that my mind is more peaceful, my heart is more open, and my relationships are more harmonious than they ever were before. I also know that before I started meditating and going to therapy, I was in a deep sleep almost all the time.

This book is a memoir about waking up to a world that's hidden deep within us and in plain sight all around us. It's also a story about meditation and psychotherapy, and how the combination of these two disciplines – one ancient and rooted in the East, the other modern and based in the West – helped me access this inner world and use what I learned there to make profound changes in both my personal and professional lives.

I wrote this book because of a need to tell my story and share it with others, with the hope that it might inspire them to look inside themselves and discover the truths that are waiting to be discovered there – and then make whatever changes are needed to live their lives in harmony with those truths.

It's never too late to start waking up. Or to find the courage to change.

For me, it all began with a chance encounter during a business trip to New York.

PART ONE
Dreamland

CHAPTER ONE

All That Glitters

I was in midtown Manhattan on a beautiful day in the summer of 1986, and I was hopelessly lost.

Not that anyone could tell. In fact, to most observers, things must have looked pretty darn good. I'd just been promoted to associate creative director at a big Boston ad agency, and I was in New York to produce a TV commercial for a computer company that was one of our biggest clients. Our campaign theme was "Take it to the Limit," and we paid big bucks for the rights to use the Eagles' hit song as our soundtrack. We also hired a top film director, a handsome young actor to play the heroic computer user, and a voice-over announcer with the deepest, most authoritative set of pipes money could buy. In short, we spared no expense, even though the spot was scheduled to run just a handful of times during an upcoming golf tournament.

Two colleagues from Boston were with me for the shoot. David, the account executive, was there to make sure we finished the job on time and on budget. And John, my art director partner and friend, was there because he, like me, wanted to end up with a commercial we could both be proud of, one we could put on our demo reels and enter into the award shows.

Day One went well. Along with the production team, we spent it on Long Island, where we shot the actor driving to work in a turbo-charged sports car and arriving at a sleek, chrome-and-glass building at the break of dawn, ready to tackle a computer-aided design problem.

But on Day Two, things started to unravel. The whole team crammed into a small studio on Fifth Avenue, ready to film our hero working at his computer and solving the problem. First, a series of glitches held up the camera crew. Then the computer wouldn't display the fancy graphics we were supposed to show off. Then the director wanted to change the lighting on the set. David kept looking at his watch, worried we were headed for costly overruns.

Shaking his head, John turned to me and whispered, "I don't like the way this is going, Tom."

"Neither do I, John."

Finally, we started filming the actor at his computer, tapping on the keyboard, looking discouraged, getting up to pace back and forth, then suddenly having an "aha moment," returning to the computer, solving the problem, and as the music swells and the Eagles sing, "Take it to the limit...one more time," raising his fist in the air and shouting, "Yeah!"

But after a dozen takes, the director still wasn't happy with the way our hero was saying his only line. So we changed it from "Yeah!" to "Yessss!" Which didn't help at all. Then the director asked if we could try "Yeah, baby!" David had concerns about that one and said he'd have to call the client for approval.

The director said, "OK, but first, let's break for lunch."

To me, the whole thing felt like a colossal waste of money and time. *My* time, in particular. As the morning dragged on, my heart kept sinking, and I knew I needed more than just a lunch break. So when David offered to take John and me to a trendy restaurant across the street, I declined, saying I needed to get some air and clear my head.

When I pushed open the heavy steel door of that overly air-conditioned studio and stepped into the summer sun, I was filled with a sense of freedom and relief. Suddenly, I was alive again. I could breathe. I could walk. I could sense a connection to the real world, not the artificial one we were creating in the studio. And as I strolled down Fifth Avenue, I put that all behind me. I had no idea where I was going. Or that I was about to stumble upon something that would change my life.

Although I'd already been on a bunch of business trips to Manhattan, I was still amazed by the scene that unfolds there during the weekday lunch hour: The hordes of humanity filling the sidewalks, the aromas of sausages and falafel wafting from the vending carts, the honking yellow cabs jockeying for position, the bicycle messengers weaving in and out of traffic, the endless game of chicken between pedestrians and vehicles at every intersection. It was exhilarating and overwhelming.

After walking through this barely controlled chaos for a few blocks, I was surprised to spot an unpretentious, funky looking bookstore, right there on fashionable Fifth Avenue. A Buddha statue sat peacefully in the window, and the books on display had alternative, spiritually oriented themes. Since I was interested in spiritual paths that felt more simpatico to me than the strict Roman Catholic faith I grew up with, I decided to go in. Maybe, I thought, this little shop could provide whatever I was looking for.

When I opened the door, I was greeted by the tinkling of a bell and the sounds of Native American flute music. The sweet scent of sandalwood incense filled the air. And there was just one other customer in the shop. As I started browsing and the cacophony of the city faded into the background, I said to myself, *Ah, this is more like it.*

The first book that caught my eye was *Journey of Awakening: A Meditator's Guidebook,* by Ram Dass. I had recently seen the author speak at an event in Cambridge and was impressed with his story. He began life as Richard Alpert and became a professor and colleague of Timothy Leary in the psychology department at Harvard in the 1960s. Together, they shared an interest in expanding human consciousness and were researching the effects of hallucinogenic drugs, including psilocybin and LSD. Although not illegal at the time, these drugs were controversial, and as a result of their work both men were dismissed from the Harvard faculty – in Alpert's case for providing drugs to an undergraduate. Leary went west to San Francisco, where he advised the young seekers gathered there to "Turn on, tune in, and drop out." And Alpert headed east to India, where he discovered the power of meditation and studied with a guru who gave him a new name: Ram Dass.

I was familiar with his countercultural classic, *Be Here Now,* but had never heard of *Journey of Awakening.* As I leafed through it in the bookstore, I realized it was filled with tales of his meditative journeys, along with advice on how to develop a personal meditation practice. And I thought, *Hmm, maybe that's what I need to get out of this funk I've been in.* So I brought it to the cashier and whipped out my credit card.

When I returned to Boston after the TV shoot, I was reminded that disillusionment with my career wasn't my only problem. My personal life was also a mess. Two years earlier, my short-lived first marriage ended in a painful divorce. Then, after a year of self-imposed celibacy, I got involved with Chloe, a fun-loving, free-spirited woman seven years younger than I who liked taking me to punk bars in Kenmore Square and watching *Pee-wee's Playhouse* with me on Saturday mornings. I was smitten. But a few weeks before my trip to New York, Chloe ended our relationship for reasons that are still unclear. It all started on a Friday night when she didn't show up for our dinner date at a local sushi place. I called her from a pay phone, left a message, and when I still hadn't heard back by Sunday morning, I walked over to her Beacon Hill apartment and rang the bell.

"Who is it?" asks the familiar voice on the intercom.

"It's me, Tom, and we need to talk."

"Okay, I'll be down in a minute."

When Chloe appears ten minutes later, her hair still wet from the shower, I suggest we walk to the nearby Boston Public Garden and find a place to talk. As soon as we sit down on an empty bench, Chloe pulls out a cigarette. Chloe smokes Mores, which are wrapped in brown paper instead of the traditional white and targeted at young, independent women. Their slogan is "Dare to be More." They also happen to be the brand my ex-wife smokes. About a month earlier, I introduced Chloe to my parents over dinner at a Harvard Square restaurant, and when she went to the ladies' room all my mother could say was, "I can't believe she smokes those same awful brown cigarettes that Arielle does!"

As Chloe lights her cigarette and takes a deep drag, I turn to her and ask, trying to sound as neutral as possible, "So what's going on? You didn't show up for sushi Friday night. I left you a message, and you didn't call back."

"I know," she says as she blows out some smoke. "I really don't know what's going on. I...I mean, I just don't think I can do this anymore."

"Do what?"

"Be in this relationship."

When I ask why, she says something about feeling tied down, not knowing who she is anymore. She tells me she freaked out when I introduced her to my parents and was surprised more recently when

I suggested the possibility of the two of us living together. I try to backpedal this suggestion by saying that it was just a thought, that we can slow down and keep things casual. But she doesn't want to hear it, or maybe she just doesn't believe it. Anyway, she says her mind is made up. And she sums up her position with a concise statement that expresses just how constrained she's been feeling in our relationship and how much she wants to be free.

"I'm not Doris Day, you know."

Ouch! That one hurt. But was it the whole story? I'll never know. It was clear, however, that I had to let her go. This not only broke my heart, but also caused me to sink into a state of anxious depression. Normally a neat freak, I let the floors of my South End condo become littered with unopened mail, dirty clothes, and dust bunnies. I had trouble sleeping most nights. I was even staying home from work on days when I didn't feel up to going in, which wasn't like me at all.

Fortunately, when my marriage was floundering, I started seeing a therapist in an effort to figure out why I was having so much trouble finding and staying in a committed, long-term relationship. And the therapy was helping. Jonathan wasn't much older than I, but he seemed more confident, more comfortable in his own skin, and wiser about the intricacies of the human heart. Like most therapists, he was also a good listener. Which I appreciated. But I wanted someone who could do more than just listen. I wanted guidance and advice, and those were two things he stubbornly refused to provide.

"Maybe I should call Chloe and give her another chance," I suggested to him one day, still grieving her loss a couple of months after she broke up with me. "What do you think?"

"I don't know," he said matter-of-factly as he gazed out the window. Then he turned, looked right at me, and added, "What do *you* think?"

"I really don't know," I shrugged. "That's why I'm asking you."

He sat back in his leather recliner and sighed. "Look," he finally said. "You keep asking me what you should do and how you should feel. It's like you keep throwing me the ball. And that's fine. That's apparently what you need to do. But my job, as your therapist, isn't to take the ball and run with it. My job is to catch the ball, take a good look at it, and toss it back to you."

This wasn't what I wanted to hear. In fact, I found his reticence frustrating and, at times, infuriating. But I didn't say anything. I just let it sink in. And gradually, through our work together, I began to understand why I always deferred to the opinions and expectations of others, and how this tendency had been shaped by childhood experiences as the first-born son in an upwardly mobile but insecure Italian American family. I saw how keenly attuned I was to the hopes and dreams of my ambitious parents and my immigrant grandparents, who had sacrificed and worked hard so their progeny could have better lives. This legacy created a strong need to please my elders, even if it was at my own expense. Working with a family therapist like Jonathan helped me see how I had been groomed to seek the approval of not only my parents, but just about everyone else. Not coincidentally, in the ad biz, my job involved literally seeking approval from others – the creative director, the account team, the client, the consumers, the award show judges.

The problem was, this tendency to keep my eye on the audience meant I often didn't know what I was feeling or what I wanted for myself.

I remember after one therapy session I went to the deli next door to get a sandwich. As I was staring up at the menu on the wall, the guy behind the counter asked me, "What'll it be?"

"I don't know," I said. "What do *you* like?"

Clearly, this problem wasn't going be an easy thing to change. And I was impatient. Yes, the therapy was helping. But to make real progress, I knew I needed something, or maybe a number of things, I could do on my own in between my weekly therapy sessions. I had already joined a gym and was working out several times a week, which helped boost my mood, at least temporarily. And when I opened up *Journey of Awakening,* I realized it was about a practice that could lead to even more profound, and more lasting, changes.

In his book, Ram Dass describes his journey from Harvard to India, from professor to spiritual seeker. He also describes different types of meditation and tells inspiring tales of where they all can lead – to wisdom, compassion, inner transformation, freedom, harmony with the universe and, ultimately, to enlightenment. Or as he puts it more poetically: a state where one "is free to enter into the ocean of love that has no beginning or end – love that is clear like a diamond, flowing like the ocean, passionate as the height of the sexual act, and soft like the caress of the wind."

That sounded pretty good to me.

Of all the meditative paths he writes about, the one I found myself drawn to was mindfulness meditation, also known as insight meditation or vipassana. It's a practice that involves anchoring your attention primarily on the sensations of breathing, but also noticing the other sensations that show up in the body, as well as the thoughts and feelings that arise in the mind and the heart – without getting lost in them. That's the tricky part. Not identifying with or getting lost in those seductive thoughts and feelings. Instead, you can simply be aware of them and watch them arise and pass away. *Journey of Awakening* suggests that if you want to become a practitioner of insight meditation, you should start out by focusing mainly on the breath and commit to practicing twice a day for at least twenty minutes each time. It also suggests practicing for thirty days before coming to any conclusions. So I decided to give it a go and to reserve any judgment about how I was doing or whether the meditation was "working." I'd stick with it for a month and then look back to see if any positive changes had taken place.

It was an easy decision to make. My girlfriend had just dumped me, and I had extra time to play with. Practicing meditation felt like a good way to spend it. So I bought a meditation cushion, set it up next to my bed, and started meditating twenty minutes each morning when I got up and twenty minutes every evening before I went to bed. At first, nothing seemed to be happening. I definitely noticed that my attention was jumping all over the place instead of staying focused on the breath sensations at the tip of my nose, which was what I wanted it to do. This was surprisingly frustrating. But I did my best to stick with it, and to remember to bring my mind back to the breath whenever I realized it had taken a trip back to my childhood or ahead to the presentation I was making to a prospective new client later that day. In fact, the only unusual thing I remember is that as the month went on, little droplets of blood began showing up at the tips of my nostrils when I wiped them with a tissue after my meditation sessions. This was vaguely troubling, but also fascinating. Was it a result of all the attention I was focusing on that area like a laser beam? I didn't know. And still don't.

What I did know at the end of those thirty days was that I felt more relaxed and more present in my life. Less anxious and depressed. I had also cleaned up my condo. I was no longer obsessing about Chloe or Arielle. And much to my surprise, I was starting to look forward to those daily meditation breaks.

My meditation practice also led to positive changes in my work with Jonathan. Although not a meditator himself, he was supportive of my newfound interest in looking within. For as I looked inside myself, in addition to sensations of breathing, I was discovering a complex world of thoughts, feelings and memories I'd been keeping at bay for most of my life. Before I started meditating, whenever I'd describe a difficult encounter at work or a painful childhood experience, Jonathan would ask, "And how do you *feel* about that?" My usual response was usually a blank stare or a shrug. "I don't know," I'd say. And I really didn't. But after I'd been meditating for a few months, I was able to say, at least some of the time, "Angry." Or "Hurt." Or even, "I feel numb."

I was also getting better at *expressing* some of those feelings. A big turning point came when I was telling Jonathan about an incident that occurred earlier that week. I was driving alone in my car one afternoon listening to a song by the Pet Shop Boys. In the chorus the singer keeps asking, apparently to the woman who just left him, *"What have I, what have I, what have I done to deserve this?"* And when I heard it that day, I suddenly remembered that my mother used that same phrase whenever my brother Paul and I were making too much noise or arguing, as brothers often do, and she was tired of listening to it. "Dear God in heaven, what have I done to deserve this?" she'd repeat in a desperate, pleading voice with her eyes turned up toward the sky. I also remembered how confused and hurt I felt when I heard those words. But I didn't just remember it. I actually felt it once again, more intensely than I ever had before. And as I was telling Jonathan about it, I was suddenly overwhelmed with sadness for that sensitive little boy who at some level realized his mother was saying that God had sent him down to her as a form of punishment. And I started sobbing, right there in front of God, Jonathan, and everyone.

It was the first time I'd been able to cry in nearly a decade. And even though I felt self-conscious, I knew those tears were a sign that something was changing inside me. And that the combination of meditation and psychotherapy had something to do with it.

As I continued to meditate and meet with Jonathan, other insights emerged, including the growing awareness that I didn't want to spend the rest of my life working in the glamorous but superficial world of advertising. That I wanted to find something more deeply satisfying and meaningful. But what?

At the time, another early influence was percolating in the back of my mind. During my freshman year in college, I read *The Greening of America,* by Charles Reich, a Yale professor who embraced the values of America's growing counterculture movement. Reich's book inspired me with its vision of a new, more humanistic, and less materialistic society. One that's built around cooperation, not competition, and that respects the needs of each individual as well as the importance of protecting the environment. Although I never considered becoming a hippie or moving to a commune, I was deeply touched by Reich's vision, and I wanted to be part of the revolution he saw coming.

So what was I doing in the advertising business? What happened to my youthful aspirations? Had I simply sold out to the seductive powers of capitalism? The more I thought about that last question, the more I had to admit that the answer was yes. But I had no idea what to do about it. The longer I was in therapy, however, the more I began to suspect that the answer was literally sitting right there in front of me, staring me in the face. Although part of me resisted the notion with all my might, I realized that if I really wanted to, I could become a therapist like Jonathan, and that this might be a better way to spend the rest of my time on this planet. I even thought I might be able find a way to combine my interests in meditation and psychotherapy.

Of course, I knew that such a change of direction would mean a huge drop in income and an uncertain future. It would also mean disappointing my parents and extended family, who were proud of the professional success I'd achieved up to that point. The more I sat with it, however, the more I came to believe it was something I needed to do. But nagging doubts kept rattling around in the back of my mind: Would I be any good as a psychotherapist? Would I even like it? And did I have the guts to go through with such a major change in my life?

Perhaps an even more important question was this: How had I become so thoroughly lost in the first place? And for the answer to that one, we need to go back a few years.

CHAPTER TWO

A Prisoner of Childhood

It's a spring day in 1960 and I'm sitting next to my brother Paul in the back seat of our parents' Oldsmobile 88, cruising down Memorial Drive with the windows open. I'm six years old, and Paul is four. We're both giggling as the breeze blows in on our faces and hair. When we pass a big gray building with pillars and a dome, my father, who recently completed his BA in accounting by attending night classes at Northeastern, points to it and says, in a tone of awe and admiration, "That's MIT. The Massachusetts Institute of Technology. It's one of the best colleges in the whole country!"

Paul and I look at the building and don't know what to make of it.

A few minutes later, as we pass the ivy-covered, red brick halls of Harvard College on our right and Harvard Business School on our left, Dad sticks his hand out the window, points and says, "And this is Harvard University. Harvard is one of the best damn schools in the whole world!"

We look again but have nothing to say.

Then my mother turns around, smiles at the two of us and says, with much enthusiasm, "Wouldn't you boys like to go there someday?"

At that point in my young life, I wanted to be a cowboy when I grew up, like Roy Rogers and the other Western heroes I saw on TV, and I had only a vague sense of what going to college might mean. But I knew for sure when I heard those words that if I could get into one of those schools someday, especially the one with the ivy and the red bricks, it would make my mother and father very proud. And very happy.

My parents were dedicated and well-intentioned parents, but like most people, they had their share of insecurities and resentments. My mother was a talented, attractive, intelligent woman who put aside any dreams she may have had about leading a more glamorous life when she gave birth to me in 1953 and became a housewife. From that point on, the only glamor in her life was related to her appearance. Always well-dressed, she had an appointment every Friday at the local beauty parlor to have her hair done. And she dyed that hair blonde in the early '60s when the folks at Clairol launched their ad campaign that coyly asked, *"Is it true blondes have more fun?"* while showing lots of blondes having lots of fun. Soon after that, when contact lenses became widely available, she didn't hesitate to trade in her glasses for a pair.

She also paid lots of attention to the way Paul and I looked. She'd tell us not to get our clothes dirty when we went out to play, which cramped our style. Like the time we were playing with Lenny and Jay Richards in their backyard. I think we were digging for buried treasure under their swing set. The Richards boys could get as dirty as they wanted, and they really got into the digging while Paul and I held back. After we'd been at it for a while, Mrs. Richards came out to check on us. She saw her kids, who looked like filthier versions of Pigpen from the old Peanuts cartoons, then looked at Paul and me, who were almost as spotless as we'd been when we left our house. She shook her head, chuckled to herself and asked us, with a sense of wonder in her voice, "How do you two stay so clean?" I just shrugged and said, "Our mother doesn't like it when we get dirty."

I was in third grade around that time and was having trouble seeing the blackboard at school. When my mother was informed of this by my teacher, she took me to an eye doctor who prescribed my first pair of glasses. But she was clearly disappointed. "Now no one will be able to see your long eyelashes," she sighed.

When I was in junior high and all the boys were letting their hair grow long like the Beatles and the Monkees, she wanted me to comb mine down over my forehead so I could have cute-looking bangs, "like your brother Paul," who by then was clearly the better-looking brother. But my hair was thinner than Paul's and it wouldn't cooperate. Around the same time, acne pimples started showing up on my face, and my mother whisked me off to a dermatologist, who prescribed antibiotics and put me on a special diet I stuck to throughout my adolescence, even though it didn't seem to help much. Then, when I was a freshman in high school, she wanted me to get my own set of contact lenses, which I resisted but finally agreed to do about halfway through my senior year. Part of me knew that my mother was doing her best to take care of me. And I never doubted that she loved me. But another part of me felt that whenever she looked at me, she was at least mildly disappointed.

By focusing her gaze on others and insisting she always knew best, my mother was able to avoid looking at her own insecurities. My father, on the other hand, was more introspective and often seemed unsure of himself. At five-foot-seven, he was on the short side, which troubled him, as did his steadily receding hairline, which began its retreat when he was in his early twenties. And like most men of his generation, he left the child-rearing decisions to his wife and preferred to focus on his career, where he enjoyed some clear success.

He was also a sports fan and followed all the Boston teams, especially the Red Sox and the Patriots. As soon as I was old enough, he explained the rules of the games to me when we watched them on TV and showed me how to read the box scores in the newspaper the next day. I became a fan, too, and looked forward to occasional outings with Dad and Paul to Fenway Park. I also liked playing baseball and football with the other boys in the neighborhood. And since I was one of the older kids, I could be a standout. This changed dramatically, however, when I tried out for Little League and had to compete against boys from all over town who were my age or even older. Instead of making a Little League team, I was relegated to the Farm League, and even in that less competitive arena I struck out a lot and made plenty of errors in the field.

Although Mom seemed disappointed in my appearance and Dad was let down by my lack of athletic prowess, they both knew I was smart. And when I brought home report cards with all A's, they were thrilled. Soon they started asking me what I wanted to be when I grew up. I didn't know what to say, but I knew it was something that mattered to them. Eventually, I got the feeling they hoped I'd become either a doctor or a priest. From a very young age, I sensed they wanted me to become someone they could show off to family and friends. Someone who could help them feel better about who they were and where they'd come from. Like the President of the United States or the first American Pope. But that would be too much to hope for. A successful doctor or beloved priest would do just fine.

Looking back on it now, I can understand where they were coming from. They were born in the late 1920s on the eve of the Great Depression. Each was the first-born child of Italian immigrants who fled conditions of extreme poverty to seek their fortunes in America. But life here wasn't much better, especially at first. My two grandfathers arrived as unmarried men in their late teens with no money and few prospects, so they relied on relatives and friends – their *paesani* – to feed them, house them, and help them get jobs. Soon, they both found work at Leopold Morse & Company, a clothing manufacturer in Boston. My paternal grandfather, a skilled tailor and the more ambitious of the two, was eventually promoted to shop foreman. My other grandfather spent his long days, which turned into four long decades, on the shop floor, sewing sleeves onto suit jackets and overcoats, over and over and over again. Although they didn't know each other at the time, they both lived in the North End, Boston's Italian ghetto, where they met two young women who had emigrated with their own families from Italy. Eventually the two couples married and moved to Italian enclaves in the nearby city of Somerville, where they settled down and raised their families.

Marianne Sica and Peter Pedulla, my parents, first crossed paths at Somerville High School, where they shared an interest in music. She was an accomplished pianist; he played clarinet and tenor sax. Pete was a year older and when he graduated, World War II was still raging. So he enlisted in the Coast Guard, hoping to stay close to American shores. What he didn't realize was that when our nation is at war, the Coast Guard is charged with guarding coastlines and supporting our troops wherever they've been deployed. So he ended up spending a year on a supply ship in the Pacific. This meant leaving home – away from his mother's apron strings and his father's nasty temper – which helped him make the transition from adolescence to adulthood. For the rest of his life, he loved telling tales of his time in the service, which included a stint in the Navy during the Korean War. These stories featured a self-effacing kind of humor, and he usually brought them out at large family gatherings when he wanted to regale a distant cousin, somebody's new boyfriend, or anyone else who hadn't heard them before.

"I signed up for the Coast Guard," he'd begin, "but I was worried they'd turn me down. Why? Because you had to weigh at least 125 pounds, and I only weighed 120. So the week before the physical, I stuffed myself at every meal. I had bacon and eggs for breakfast, salami sandwiches for lunch, second and third helpings of pasta at dinner time, two scoops of ice cream for dessert, and milkshakes in between meals. By the end of the week, I was up to 126. I was ready! But when I stripped down for my physical and stepped on the scale, it said 123. I couldn't believe it! I looked at the sergeant, and he looked back at me. Then he made a face, put his foot on the scale, and we both watched the little red needle shoot up to 129. "One-hundred-and-twenty-nine pounds," he shouted as he wrote it down. "Congratulations, kid. You're in!"

When the war ended, Pete returned home, reconnected with Marianne, and together with some friends they formed a 10-piece big band. "Marianne and her Orchestra" was a popular dance band that played at ballrooms and other venues in the Boston area during the late '40s and early '50s. It was an exciting time for them. And the excitement involved more than just making music together. They also fell in love. The couple married in 1952 and continued to play local gigs and dream of making the big time, at least until I was born about eighteen months later.

That's when everything changed. The young couple, along with their newborn son, moved from their tiny studio apartment to the first floor of a two-family house owned by my father's parents, who lived upstairs. Pete, who held various odd jobs to supplement the income generated by the band, realized it was time to get serious and find a career. So he enrolled at a junior college and majored in accounting. And Marianne, who'd been working as a medical secretary, became a stay-at-home mom.

According to my parents, I was a colicky baby who cried a lot, especially at night, which created stress in the household and elicited some not-so-helpful advice from my grandmother. "Just let him cry himself to sleep," she insisted, "he's got to learn." This was the conventional wisdom at the time, and my mother gave it a try. Although I can't say exactly how this affected me, I know that getting a good night's sleep has always been one of my challenges, as has trusting anyone who claims to be a caregiver.

Two years later, Paul was born, and the young couple – especially my mother – decided it was time to move out of my grandparents' house. This was understandable, for while Pete was busy working and going to school, Marianne was not only stuck in the house with an infant and a toddler, but also was under the constant scrutiny of her mother-in-law. I remember my grandmother as a wonderful cook and a loving presence who helped take care of Paul and me when we lived on the first floor of her house. But she had a way of making Marianne feel inadequate as a mother and not quite good enough for my father, who, in his mother's eyes, could do no wrong.

Another two years went by, and my parents were finally able to buy a house in the small town of Chelmsford, about 25 miles northwest of Boston. Our new home was a three-bedroom ranch in a new neighborhood full of identical three-bedroom ranches, with a few Cape Cod style houses thrown in to break up the monotony. Because the neighborhood was built on land that had been a family farm, there was plenty of open space where kids could run around and play. Almost all the homeowners were new to town, and most had kids around the same ages as Paul and me. So it was a good place to grow up, and I was happy to be there. But my paternal grandfather never quite forgave my parents for moving so far away. "What do you want to move there for?" he'd grumble. "Chelmsford is way out in the sticks!" He'd conveniently forgotten that he moved thousands of miles away from his own parents when he was a young man. But he was angry and hurt that his son's family left the home he'd been providing for us.

We'd still visit Nonno and Nonna Pedulla in Somerville most weekends, but they seldom made the drive to Chelmsford to visit us. And whenever they did, there was tension in the air. My grandmother would bring eggplant parmigiana or another special dish she prepared for the occasion, which she'd deliver with a mixed message.

"I made this for Peter," she'd say to my mother as she handed over the platter of food.

"Oh, thank you," my mother would reply graciously. But as soon as her mother-in-law was out of earshot, she'd mutter to herself and to anyone close enough to hear, "She made it for Peter? Can't the rest of us eat it, too?"

As time went by, we saw less and less of my father's parents, and more and more of my mother's. Nonno and Nonna Sica were happy to drive out to Chelmsford, which they did most Saturday afternoons, bearing gifts of Italian bread, cheese, wine, and other goodies my grandfather purchased on his weekly shopping trips to Boston's North End. They sometimes brought steaks, too, which my father would grill outside in the summertime for our Saturday night supper. They were delighted their daughter had married Pete, a nice Italian boy who was a good provider, and they loved him as if he were one of their own.

After supper, they'd drive back to Somerville. The next morning, after attending the 8:15 mass at St. Mary's Church, we'd all pile into my father's car and make the trek to Somerville to join Nonno and Nonna Sica for a big Sunday dinner in the triple-decker where they lived.

That rickety house was our family's version of the Kennedy compound, but instead of being spread across several acres of prime oceanfront real estate in picturesque Hyannisport, it was confined to a postage-stamp piece of asphalt in hardscrabble Somerville, or as it was known back then, "Slumerville." Somehow, my great-grandparents managed to scrape together enough money to buy the house, and my great-grandmother still lived on the first floor. My grandparents were on the second floor. And my grandmother's younger sister, my great aunt Clara, lived on the third floor with her three grown children: Joe (a.k.a. "Sonny"), Rosemarie and Alfred.

When we were little, Paul and I looked forward to these weekly pilgrimages. They felt exotic and other worldly, nothing like our lives in suburban, white-bread Chelmsford. At the same time, they had a familiar, almost ritualized quality. Each week, before we went upstairs to see my grandparents, we'd stop to say hello to my great-grandmother on the first floor. She was a tiny but imposing figure who still owned and ruled over the family compound. In fact, my cousin Rosemarie called her "the Inspector General." Paul and I called her "Big Nonna," and our visits with her were brief. Although she'd lived in the U.S. for nearly forty years by then, she was always surrounded by native Italians and never learned to speak English. My mother would knock on her door, and Big Nonna, clad in a simple cotton housedress with her white hair pulled back into a bun, would appear in her doorway and begin speaking to my parents in Italian. Then she'd turn to Paul and me, tussle our hair or pinch our cheeks, and continue chatting with my parents.

"What'd she say, what'd she say?" we'd demand.

"She said you're cute but you're still too skinny," my mother would reply.

Each week we'd make this obligatory stop, pay our respects, and Big Nonna would give us her blessing and seal of approval. Then we'd say goodbye and climb the winding staircase to see my grandparents on the second floor. Here, there was no need to knock. The door was always open, and we'd just walk right in. My grandmother would be at the stove or the sink getting dinner ready. My grandfather would be sitting in his rocking chair reading the Sunday paper or mending some socks. My mother would offer to help with dinner, and if the offer was refused, as it usually was, she'd sit down at the kitchen table with my father and chat with my grandparents, while I'd feel my appetite spike as I inhaled the tantalizing aromas from the nearby oven and stovetop.

Soon, Auntie Clara and one or more of her offspring would come downstairs to say hello and join the conversation. Paul and I would be thrilled if Sonny or Alfred showed up. They were big, strapping, fun-loving guys who were younger than our parents but much older than us. "Hey, it's the Pedulla boys!" they'd shout as they walked in. "How you guys doin'?" Then they'd talk about sports, tell jokes, and devise other ways to amuse their little cousins. As a couple of single, seemingly carefree, working-class guys who had taken over their father's trucking business when he died, they had a spontaneity and lack of pretentiousness about them that was refreshing. They'd hang out and entertain us for a while, then go off to do whatever it was they had planned for the rest of the day.

Dinner was always a feast. We'd start with macaroni (which we'd later learn to call "pasta") and homemade "gravy" (which we'd learn to call "sauce") along with the accompanying "gravy meat": meatballs, sausages, braciola, and a few pieces of chicken thrown in for extra flavor. This would be followed by a second course, usually a roast of some kind, with various vegetables and a big garden salad on the side. After dinner, there was fruit and, of course, coffee and dessert, which could be a homemade sponge cake, Italian pastries from the local bakery, or just some ice cream, Jell-O or pudding.

Try as we might, Paul and I could never eat enough to satisfy my grandmother. "Have some more," she'd say whenever she noticed our plates were empty. We'd refuse, rubbing our bellies and proclaiming we were too full, but she'd override our objections and plop down another helping anyway.

"It does my heart good to see you eat like this," she'd say, with a big smile on her face and a look of satisfaction in her eyes. And we'd force ourselves to eat a little more.

After dinner, the men would adjourn to the living room to watch the Red Sox game or whatever else was on TV, and the women would return to the kitchen to do the dishes and talk. Eventually, my parents would say it was time to leave, and we'd kiss everyone goodbye before making the quick trip across town to pay our respects to Nonno and Nonna Pedulla. These visits were briefer and less memorable but were generally pleasant enough – except for one recurring, hair-related problem. Nonno Pedulla, in addition to being a skilled tailor, was a semi-professional barber. As a boy back in Italy, he contributed to his family's meager income by visiting the local farmers and cutting their hair. Now that he was no longer providing shelter for our family, he figured he could at least save my parents a few bucks by giving free haircuts to my father, Paul, and me. For the first few years, we were willing to submit to his clippers. But as we got older and more concerned about our looks, Paul and I began to resist. Paul was especially adamant that he didn't want Nonno cutting his hair anymore. My grandfather eventually got the message, but this rejection just added more distance to a relationship that was already strained.

As Paul and I began developing our own sets of friends and interests, these weekly visits to Somerville became less appealing and less frequent. My parents' lives also became more complicated by the arrival of two more children. After three miscarriages in the late '50s and early '60s, my mother gave birth to my brother Pete in 1963 and sister Maryellen in 1966. Another turning point came in 1967, when my parents sold their three-bedroom ranch and built a large, four-bedroom colonial for their growing family in a more upscale section of Chelmsford.

Life was good, at least on the surface. My father was climbing the corporate ladder, and we were an upwardly mobile family. We were making it in America. But underneath it all, there was a craving for more, a nagging hope that things could be even better. Some of this hope was projected onto me, the eldest child and first grandchild on both sides of the family.

Years later, when I was in therapy with Jonathan and he was helping me understand the pressure to achieve I felt as a child and continued to experience as an adult, he suggested I read a book called *Prisoners of Childhood: The Drama of the Gifted Child and the Search for the True Self,* by the Swiss psychoanalyst Alice Miller. In this classic text, Miller describes the problems that ensue when "gifted" – meaning sensitive and empathic – children become overly attuned to their parents' needs for affirmation and self-esteem. These children then take it upon themselves to try to meet those needs, which is impossible, for such needs must first be met at a much earlier stage in a person's development. The problem here is that in their valiant attempt to take care of their parents, these children put their own emotional needs aside. They become especially adept at suppressing their darker emotions – like anger, fear, and sadness – which are a vital part of any mentally healthy, emotionally mature, fully functioning adult.

Jonathan suspected that I was one of those "gifted" children. Although I didn't agree with him at the time, I eventually came to see that his diagnosis was almost certainly correct.

CHAPTER THREE

The Trauma of the Gifted Child

Transitioning from life in Somerville to life in Chelmsford must have been a huge challenge for my mother. True, she was no longer under the surveillance of her mother-in-law. Instead, she was alone in the wilderness. Like most car-owning families in 1958, we had just one. So except on the occasional days when she'd drive my father to work, she was stuck in a little ranch house with two young sons and no way to escape. She couldn't walk or take a bus to the grocery store or beauty parlor, like she used to do in Somerville. She didn't have friends or relatives nearby. She was no longer working for a prominent Boston obstetrician. In what was perhaps the biggest blow of all, she was no longer the "Marianne" of Marianne and her Orchestra, the only woman in the band and in many ways the star of the show.

Like most women of her generation, she gave it all up to become a housewife and mother, two jobs she pursued with a passion. And if she had a hard time accepting her diminished status and remote location, she did her best not to let it show. She reached out to her new neighbors and made new friends. She became an excellent cook, and when some of the neighbors entered a baking contest sponsored by WCAP, the local radio station, she joined them and took home the grand prize: a brand new stove!

Despite my mother's efforts to embrace her new role and remain cheerful, I could sense something lurking below the surface. Whenever my father was late getting home from work, she'd become anxious and would station me at the living room window as a lookout. "Let me know as soon as you see his car," she'd tell me, "so I can put the macaroni in." I'd sit there craning my neck, peering down the street, worried that he'd been in a fatal car accident. But eventually, his big black Oldsmobile would appear and, feeling relieved, I'd run into the kitchen shouting, "He's here…he's here!" Then I'd watch her dump a box of Prince ziti into a pot of boiling water, and all would be well. At least for a while.

She often had headaches, too, which made her irritable, especially when the weather was hot and humid. "God help me," she'd say, "I can't take another day like this." Two or three times a year, for no apparent reason, she'd also have debilitating backaches. These would force her to rest and require Paul and me to be on our best behavior and help with the dishes, the dusting, and the vacuuming. Despite these challenges, however, she always seemed to be in control and in command. With at least one memorable exception.

It was the summer of 1961. I was seven years old. A section of a new superhighway, Interstate 495, was under construction in Chelmsford. And it was happening just beyond the borders of our neighborhood. My mother told Paul and me not to go near the construction site because "it's too dangerous for children." But that just made us more curious. One day, we were hanging out with five or six of our friends, all boys about our age. And we were looking for something to do. In the distance, we heard the rumbling of the dump trucks, bulldozers, and earth movers, and it was like a siren's call.

"Let's go take a look," says Jackie Sanderson, who likes to push the envelope.

"We can't," I say. "Our mother says it's too dangerous."

"Aw, c'mon. We won't get too close."

All the other boys think this is an excellent plan. So I give in, and we make our way to the edge of the neighborhood, then go just a little further until we find a stand of trees overlooking the construction site. Below the trees there's a stream, and we're surprised to see a big turtle in it. Across from the stream, the land rises again to where the massive yellow excavators are digging up the earth and piling it into dump trucks. It feels like we're far enough away and in a safe place. And since it's one of those hot, humid days, we enjoy sitting in the shade of the trees and watching the show.

After a while, Jackie gets bored with the trucks and starts throwing rocks at the turtle.

"Cut it out, Jackie," I say. "Leave the turtle alone."

"I'm just trying to make it move," he replies as he continues throwing rocks in the turtle's direction.

"You're gonna hurt the turtle."

Just as I say this, he heaves a big one that lands on the turtle's back and cracks its shell.

Jackie starts laughing. "Bullseye!" he says.

I feel bad for the turtle and stand up to confront him. "Look what you did," I shout as I shove him with both hands. "I knew you were going to hurt that turtle!"

"So what are you going to do about it?" he snarls as he pushes me back.

This is followed by more pushing and shoving, but before it can escalate into a fight, the other boys intervene, tell us to calm down, and we go back to watching the trucks. After a while, one of our friends turns around, looks scared, points, and says, "Oh-oh." Then we all turn around and see a group of six mothers marching toward us. And they do not look happy.

Our mother seems to be the most upset. "I told you not to go near here," she hisses as she grabs Paul and me by our collars and starts walking us home. "You had me worried to death," she adds. When I feel the tightness of her grip, I know we're in trouble. She doesn't say another word during the ten-minute walk back to our house, and as her grip loosens, I hope she's calming down and things won't be so bad. But once we get inside, she slams the door behind us, throws us to the floor, and starts hitting us harder than she ever has before. "Don't you ever…" (WHACK!) "disobey me…" (WHACK!) "again!" (WHACK! WHACK!) "Do you know how worried I was about you?" (WHACK! WHACK!! WHACK!!!)

The beating seems to go on forever. I'm terrified and disoriented. I've never seen her in such a state and don't know what to make of it. Paul and I are both wailing and begging her to stop, which she finally does. The two of us are lying on the floor, still sobbing, while she remains standing over us, breathing heavily. "Now go to your room," she commands as she points toward the bedroom we share, "while I figure out what your punishment is going to be."

Back then, corporal punishment was still a common practice in American households. "Spare the rod and spoil the child" was considered sound advice by many, if not most, parents. So Paul and I were used to getting occasional slaps on our backsides from my mother's hand, or, for more serious offenses, from her wooden spoon. These were light blows that weren't intended to hurt us, but to get our attention and interrupt something she considered to be bad behavior.

However, what happened on that summer day was of a different order of magnitude, and it shook me to the core. As I lay on my bed and my sobbing subsided, I resolved that I would never do anything to make my mother upset like that again.

After my father got home and the two of them discussed the incident, we were allowed to emerge from our room so we could face our sentence. For the next two weeks, Paul and I were both grounded, which meant we couldn't venture beyond the limits of our quarter-acre lot. This seemed harsh to us, especially the next day, when we learned that none of our friends were being punished at all. "Well, they can play with you over here," my mother said, "but you two *cannot* leave this yard." We thought this was unfair, but there was no higher court to which we could appeal. After a couple of days, however, when our parents saw how unhappy and repentant we were, they reduced our sentence to just one week.

To her credit, my mother never beat us like that again. In fact, I'm pretty sure she didn't hit us even once after that day. Maybe she scared herself as much as she scared the two of us. Or maybe our behavior improved to the point where spankings were no longer necessary.

Not that we suddenly became little angels. There was at least one time after the Route 495 incident when she sent us to our room because of something we did or failed to do. I can't recall what it was. But I clearly remember what followed. "Just wait till your father hears about this," she warned us. We went to our room and waited, wondering what our fate would be. When my father got home, we heard him talking with my mother in the kitchen. Then he opened the door to our bedroom and stormed in. "Your mother told me what you boys did today," he said, trying to sound outraged as he pulled off his belt and held it high over his head, ready to strike. He had threatened us with his belt a few times before but had never actually used it. But this time felt different. We both cowered and looked down at the floor as he held the belt over us, poised to deliver the first blow. Then there was a pause. We finally looked up at him and he looked down at us. Somehow, when our eyes met, we all knew he wasn't going to hit us with that belt, with his hand, or with anything else – not then, not ever. I don't remember who smiled first, but one of us did, and pretty soon we were all smiling and giggling, and he was putting his belt back on and saying, "Look, just try to be good and don't upset your mother, OK?"

Despite occasional threats, my father never hit us for any reason, which is surprising when you consider that his own father didn't hesitate to use physical violence to keep his three sons in line. One Sunday when we were visiting Nonno and Nonna Pedulla, my father pointed out the thick, black leather sharpening strop that hung from a hook on the back of their bathroom door. "That's what your grandfather beat us with when we were bad," he told us in a hushed voice. I shuddered to think about what it must have felt like to be struck with such an instrument of torture. And I was glad my father somehow decided that the cycle of violence would end with him.

CHAPTER FOUR

My Mother the Doctor, My Father the Priest

My mother had a strong interest in all things medical. She was proud of her days as a medical secretary, and she liked to keep up with all the latest medical news and trends. If she'd been born a generation or two later, she might have become a doctor herself. And she probably would have been a good one. She was quite skilled at diagnosing our childhood illnesses and taking care of us whenever we were sick or injured. I always felt like I was in good hands when I was hurting, whether it was because of something minor like a scraped knee or a head cold, or something more serious like chicken pox or a broken bone.

One day when I was about eight years old, I was in a neighbor's yard playing army with my friends. We divided ourselves into two forces – the Japs and the Americans – and were fighting for control of the "Big Rock," a giant boulder at the edge of the neighbor's yard. Our weapons were toy guns that made lots of noise but didn't actually shoot anything, and the rules weren't exactly clear about how one side would defeat the other. We were just having fun. But then Larry White, who tended to get carried away, got on top of the Big Rock and started throwing smaller rocks at the enemy below. One of those rocks landed on top of my head. It didn't hurt much, but I was pissed off and started lecturing Larry about throwing rocks at people, which was not a safe thing to do. Instead of arguing with me, Larry just stared, pointed to my head and said, with a look of horror on his face, "The blood...the blood!" I reached up with my hand and felt my head, which was warm and wet. Then I looked at my hand and was horrified to see it covered with bright red blood. Instantly, I started to cry, then dropped my gun and went running home to mother.

By the time I got there, the blood was running down my neck onto my shirt, and I was wailing. I was in a state of panic, thinking I might have been mortally wounded. "Mommy, mommy," I yelled when I arrived. She met me at the back door, and although she must have been shocked at the sight of her little boy covered in blood, she remained calm and handled the situation like a pro. She asked me what happened, and I told her. As soon as we got inside, she grabbed a towel, wiped up as much blood as she could, and told me I was going to be okay. Then she wrapped another towel around my head, called our neighbor across the street, and asked her to drive us to the hospital. In practically no time, we were in the emergency room at Lowell General, and a doctor was shaving the area around the cut, stitching it closed, and assuring my mother and me that I was going to be just fine, but that I should take it easy for the rest of the day.

When we got home, she told me to lie down and rest while she made my favorite lunch, grilled cheese and tomato soup, which she put on a tray and brought to me in bed.

Throughout my childhood, what eventually became even more obvious than my mother's diagnostic and clinical skills, along with her excellent bedside manner, was the high esteem in which she held almost all doctors, especially the "good ones." She'd speak in reverent tones about the obstetrician she used to work for, the one who delivered Paul and me. "He's such a wonderful man," she'd gush, "so dedicated and so professional. They don't make 'em like that anymore."

She also made an effort to choose the best possible doctors for herself and her family. She was delighted when she found the man who became our family pediatrician. Not only did Dr. Klein know his stuff, but he was also intelligent, witty, and good with kids. This was back when doctors made house calls, and whenever Dr. Klein came to see Paul or me, he'd bring along some balloons and jokes to entertain us – that "spoonful of sugar" to help the medicine go down. And when my brother Pete and sister Maryellen came along, he became their pediatrician, too. But as she got older, Maryellen said she didn't feel comfortable with him, and my mother agreed to find a different doctor for her. At first, I thought Mel was being overly fussy. Then, a year or so later, we were all shocked to read in the local paper that Dr. Klein had been accused of sexual misconduct by several of his young female patients.

Despite this disturbing news, my mother's respect for the medical profession remained strong, and as I got older, she'd sometimes ask if I ever thought about becoming a doctor, which she obviously thought would be a wonderful thing. I didn't know what to say, but I did consider pursuing a career in medicine, even though I wasn't interested in any of the material I'd have to study along the way. I finally put the idea to rest during my freshman year in college, when my lowest grade was in intro biology, and I couldn't imagine getting through the advanced chemistry and biochem courses I'd have to take before I could even apply to medical school.

My father seemed less invested in influencing my career choice, perhaps because he was so wrapped up in advancing his own career. He never pushed me to become a doctor, a lawyer, or even a corporate executive like himself. The only thing he ever pushed on me was the

Roman Catholic Church. As soon as we moved to Chelmsford, we began attending Mass every Sunday at St. Mary's, our local parish. For years, it had been a small "mission church," for there had never been many Catholics in the area. Since its founding in 1655, Chelmsford had always been very WASPish, filled with Protestant churches of all denominations. But in the '50s and '60s, the Pedulla family was part of a wave of Irish, Italian, Polish, and French-Canadian families – almost all Catholic -- who moved in and swelled the town's population from 10,000 to about 30,000. Soon, we needed a bigger church, and my father was on a committee that raised money for the new St. Mary's.

After it was built, he also became a lector, a layperson with a seat near the altar who read the weekly Epistle from the letters of St. Paul and led the parishioners in their responses to the priest. And since he was an accountant, he volunteered to do the tax returns for our parish priests, who came to our house and sat with him as he made the calculations and filled out the forms.

My father held all priests in high esteem. This feeling of respect probably began during his childhood, when he was an altar boy at St. Polycarp's in Somerville. So it's not surprising that as soon as I was old enough, he urged me to become an altar boy, too. I did this willingly, for it felt like an honor to be up there participating in the Mass, reciting prayers in Latin, and assisting the priests. Two years later, Paul also became an altar boy. And when St. Mary's formed its first boys' choir, my father encouraged us both to join. Soon, we were singing from the choir loft every Sunday morning at the 8:15 Mass.

In addition to serving as altar boys and choir boys, we attended catechism classes during the week. Initially, these were taught by local nuns, whom I found intimidating and inscrutable. Later, the classes were led by adult volunteers from the parish. These lay teachers were less threatening but not very inspiring either.

By the time I entered puberty, I was becoming disenchanted with the church. But I kept that to myself, especially since my father was so pleased that Paul and I were apparently on the road to becoming good Catholics. At one point, he even suggested that I consider a higher calling. It happened during a game of catch.

Dad and I were in the backyard tossing a baseball back and forth. He said he'd just met a young Catholic priest who was visiting the Chitticks, our next-door neighbors. After we finished, as we walked toward the house, he told me the priest was Mrs. Chittick's brother.

"It would be such a blessing to have a priest in the family," he said wistfully. "And you know, those priests have a good life. The church takes care of them, and everyone looks up to them." Then, after a pause, he put his hand on my shoulder, looked me in the eye and asked, "Have you ever thought about becoming a priest?"

This took me by surprise, for the thought had never crossed my mind. In fact, I always felt a little creepy around priests. As an altar boy, I'd see them behind the scenes. And though they'd never done anything to arouse suspicion, they didn't seem especially holy or wise or even intelligent to me. I also didn't like the way they talked down to everyone – literally and figuratively – from the pulpit. And I thought that taking a vow of celibacy seemed like a weird thing to do.

"Not really," was all I could say.

After that day, the subject was dropped. But when I was about to graduate from junior high, both parents wanted me to apply to Xavier High School, an all-boys Catholic school run by the Jesuits in nearby Concord. I had no interest in doing that and gave my parents two good reasons: First, I didn't want to go to an all-boys school. And second, Xavier didn't have a band where I could continue playing my clarinet.

As a former clarinetist and saxophonist himself, my father could appreciate that second reason. And I'm sure both parents could understand the first. So they withdrew their request, and I got ready to start ninth grade at Chelmsford High.

But my attraction to young women had started to blossom a few years before that.

CHAPTER FIVE

Not Ready for Primetime

My relationships with the other sex would become more complicated as I approached adolescence, and this became painfully clear to me toward the end of sixth grade.

About halfway through that school year, five of my classmates and I formed what could loosely be referred to as a rock band. We called ourselves the Israelites in honor of our teacher, Miss Israel. Our instrumentation – electric guitar, drums, two trumpets and two clarinets – was unconventional. But we all could sing, and most of us had at least a modicum of musical talent. In fact, two of my fellow Israelites went on to become professional musicians. Our repertoire featured songs by Herman's Hermits, the Animals and, wait for it – Mr. Wayne Newton. At our first public appearance during the annual school talent show, we won first prize. After that, we were "must-see" entertainment at all school gatherings. Like the real rock bands of the era, we even had our share of groupies. And despite my dorky glasses and shy personality, I suddenly became one of the cool kids.

Much to my surprise, a girl from Miss Bridges' class across the hall let me know she was interested in getting to know me better.

She did this by turning around and staring at me in study hall one day. With her long dark hair and big green eyes, Kathy was the prettiest girl in school, at least in my opinion. I couldn't believe my good luck, especially when, with hardly any effort on my part, we became an item. I was flattered, but I had no idea what to do with a girlfriend besides talk to her at recess and walk home with her after school. I was just eleven years old and a late bloomer, emotionally as well as physically. Born in December, I was also one of the youngest kids in my class. While some of my male classmates – like Peter, my good friend and fellow Israelite – had entered puberty, my voice hadn't yet begun to change, and the only hair on my body was on top of my head.

Like everyone else, I'd heard rumors about some of the more adventurous sixth graders playing spin the bottle at parties or "making out" in the woods near our school. But I wasn't ready for anything like that, and I didn't even suspect what it could lead to because no one had bothered to fill me in on how babies are made.

One afternoon that spring, for reasons I can't quite remember, Peter, Kathy, and her friend Ginnie, who was Peter's groupie girlfriend, all showed up at my house, and we went down to the playroom in our finished basement to hang out. No sooner had we seated ourselves on the big sofa in the corner of the room when my mother came down the stairs carrying a basket of clothes. "Hope you don't mind," she said as she put the basket down on the floor, "but I have some ironing to do." She promptly set up her ironing board, went to work, and kept chatting with us and glancing over in our direction. This didn't bother me, but the girls seemed miffed. Ginnie kept giggling and saying, "But I want to *do something*." None of us could come up with any decent ideas, so after a while, Peter and the girls left.

Later that same afternoon, my mother pulled me aside and

asked, "What do you think that girl meant when she said she wanted to *do something*?"

"I don't know," I said with a shrug. And I really didn't.

When the academic year ended, to celebrate our graduation from elementary school, our teachers took all the sixth graders on a field trip to Benson's Wild Animal Farm, a combination zoo/amusement park in Hudson, New Hampshire. Kathy, Ginnie, Peter, and I agreed to spend the day together, and I was looking forward to it. We found seats next to each other on the bus, and everything started out happily and innocently enough. I had no idea how quickly it would all unravel.

When my friends and I stepped off the bus, we breathed in the aromas of freshly popped popcorn and cotton candy, mixed with more pungent scents from the animal cages. We heard the crashing of the bumper cars and the music from the carousel in the distance. Not sure where to start, we decided to see some of the exotic animals – the lions, tigers, elephants, and gorillas – in the morning, then go on the rides and check out the other attractions in the afternoon.

After lunch, Kathy and Ginnie were walking together in front of Peter and me and leading us toward The Maze, a confusing configuration of 10-foot-high hedges that was easy to find your way into, but a challenge to find your way out of. As we approached the entrance, Peter poked me with his elbow and said, in a low voice and with a conspiratorial grin on his face, "Here we go." I had no idea what he was talking about, but I followed along. The next thing I knew, the four of us were stuck in the middle of The Maze, and the girls were suggesting we take advantage of the privacy and play a kissing game. However, there were at least two problems with this idea. Ginnie was a bit hesitant, and I was dead set against it, partly because I was afraid we'd be in trouble if we got caught, and partly because I was just plain afraid. To show us it would be fun and no big deal, Peter and Kathy snuck around a corner and pretended to smooch. I could tell they were just pretending, but the pressure to go along and do something I didn't feel comfortable doing, combined with the fact that my girlfriend Kathy appeared to be kissing my good friend Peter, was too much for me to bear. I turned around, found my way out of The Maze as quickly as possible, and didn't look back.

On the bus ride back to Chelmsford, I sat by myself, feeling lonely and confused. When I finally got home, my mother greeted me and cheerfully asked, "So how was it?" I took one look at her and started to cry. After the tears subsided, I told her what happened. She hugged me and said I did the right thing. But I wasn't so sure. I just knew that I wasn't one of the cool kids anymore and probably never would be again. And that eleven years old was a lot older than I wanted to be.

While I remain friends with Peter to this day, I'm sorry to say that I never spoke to Kathy again. This wasn't my intention. I still liked her and wasn't angry at her or anyone else for that matter. But I felt ashamed and hurt, and I was convinced the whole school knew about the incident in The Maze and was laughing at me behind my back. I just wanted to pretend the whole thing never happened. Besides, it was summer now, so I wouldn't have to see my school friends again until September, when we'd all become students in the new junior high school that was about to open.

As it turned out, Kathy wasn't in any of my junior high classes, and the same would be true when we got to Chelmsford High School two years later. I'd occasionally see her in the hallways, but we never exchanged anything more than a passing glance. I was sure she still considered me to be a hopeless wimp. Many years later, when I was still thinking about the ill-fated outing to Benson's Wild Animal Farm, it suddenly occurred to me that Kathy also might have been upset about what happened, or didn't happen, in The Maze. Maybe she was even hurt by the way I acted that day.

Anyway, during the long, hot summer after sixth grade, my parents must have discussed my ignorance about human sexuality and decided I needed to be enlightened before going on to junior high. When I was younger and asked them where babies came from, probably during one of my mother's pregnancies, they told me that when two people love each other and get married, God usually sends them children. And I took them at their word. Hey, if God created the whole universe and performed all those miracles we learned about in catechism class, sending a little baby to a nice married couple would be a piece of cake, right?

My father finally had "the talk" with me one Saturday afternoon when he was taking me home from a visit to his office in his 1962 Volkswagen Beetle. Since he was driving and we were both facing the road ahead, there was no eye contact, which made the conversation less awkward for both of us. Dad began by describing the biology and mechanics of human reproduction in strictly clinical terms, but he also emphasized the importance of love and commitment between the participants. Then he gave me the Catholic party line: Any sex outside of holy matrimony is a mortal sin, and so is masturbation. He even told me the Biblical story of Onan, who "spilled his seed" on the ground and incurred the wrath of God, who slew him. He didn't say this last part with much conviction, and I now believe he was informing me only because he thought it was his duty as a good Catholic. But everything he told me that day came as a huge surprise. It all sounded strange and a little funny to me, but I was glad, at last, to be in on the joke.

When I started junior high in the fall, I found myself in a challenging new world. The new school was much bigger than any of the elementary schools I'd attended. And instead of having one teacher

43

and staying in one classroom, we had a different teacher for each sub-ject, so we had to change classes and stop at our lockers in between to make sure we had the right books, and we had to do it all without being late for our next class. It was stressful, but I eventually got the hang of it.

I was also finally going through puberty. And I developed a major crush on a girl who was in almost all my classes. She was smart and pretty and seemed very sophisticated to me. She had a great sense of humor, too. But she also seemed way out of my league, so I never even considered revealing my feelings to her or anyone else. I didn't want to risk getting hurt or being laughed at again. But by keeping my feelings inside, my crush became an obsession. I thought about her all the time and fantasized about what it would be like if we were together, how it would feel to hold her in my arms and kiss her on the lips. This painful, unrequited love persisted throughout my two years of junior high and my first two years of high school, when my outlook, and my prospects, slowly began to improve.

CHAPTER SIX

The Highs and Lows of High School

When I entered Chelmsford High in the fall of 1967, it was a rambling, red-brick building surrounded by athletic fields, tennis courts and parking lots. Although it had been built just a decade earlier, it was overflowing with close to 2,000 students and was near the end of its useful life. Shortly after I graduated, it was converted to a second junior high when the town opened a larger, more modern high school.

My four years in high school were marked by academic achievement and social awkwardness. I got good grades, and by senior year it was clear I'd graduate near the top of my class. My scholastic success was fueled by a knack for scoring high on standardized tests, a skill that helped me become a whiz at Trivial Pursuit, as well as by a tendency to be a people pleaser and approval seeker, which helped me give my teachers what they wanted.

But as I feared in sixth grade, I never again became one of the cool kids, like the athletes or the guys who had their own cars or the ones who played in rock bands. Oh, I had plenty of friends, but they were mostly other guys who did well in school and were admired by their teachers, but not necessarily by their peers.

Girls continued to seem unapproachable and intimidating. During my junior year, I finally got over my long-term crush and found myself attracted to other girls, some of whom were sophomores and not in any of my classes. So how could I get to know them? How could I even let them know I was interested? It was all a puzzle to me.

Dating became more of a possibility when I got my driver's license during my senior year. Before that, I'd need my parents to provide the transportation, which would've been way too embarrassing to endure. But now, if I only had the nerve, I could pick a girl up and take her home myself. So I began working up the courage to call my latest crush, who was in several of my classes. She had big brown eyes and a confident air. Every time our eyes met, I felt a zap of electricity. It was so palpable I figured she had to be feeling the same thing. Or at least a similar thing. One night, with my mouth dry and my heart pounding, I picked up the phone and called her. She was surprised to hear from me, but not in a good way. When I asked if she'd like to see a movie with me that weekend, she came up with a feeble excuse, cut the conversation short, and didn't encourage me to call back.

I was devastated but not defeated. After taking a month or so to regroup, I found myself attracted to another girl. She was a year behind me, and our only connection was riding the same bus to and from school every day. I didn't know much about her, but I thought she was beautiful, and we'd occasionally say hello and smile at each other on the bus. I had no idea if she'd go out with me, but I figured it was worth a try. So one night I called her and made another movie proposal. Much to my surprise, she accepted. I was excited but also nervous. What would we talk about? Just to be safe, I made a list of possible topics and put it in my pocket. After the movie, we went out for a bite at a local pizza joint and covered several of those topics. When I drove her home, I walked her to her front door, and we exchanged a quick goodnight kiss.

Things went well, I thought, and I wanted to see her again. The senior prom was coming up, and though I wasn't planning to go, the idea of going with this particular girl on my arm was very appealing. So I called and invited her to be my date for the big event. She paused, then said she was sorry, but someone else had already asked her and she said yes.

Of course, I was disappointed. And at that point, since I didn't really want to go to the prom in the first place, I decided to skip it. No big deal. But when my mother heard the news, she was disappointed, too, and she went to work behind the scenes. A week later, she told me she'd been talking with Mrs. White, a friend from our old neighborhood and the mother of Larry White, the guy who threw the rock that hit me on the head and sent me to the hospital many years before. When the subject of the prom came up, Mrs. White allegedly said her daughter Mary would be happy to go with me.

"Oh, Mom, you shouldn't have done that," I groaned in disbelief.

"Do what? I didn't do anything," she insisted. "It was all Mrs. White's idea."

I didn't believe her for a minute, and besides, no matter whose idea it was, I didn't want to be manipulated into taking someone to the prom. "But I don't want to go to the prom with Mary White," was all I could say.

"Oh, come on," my mother said. "Mary's a very nice girl. And unlike that other girl you asked, she wants to go with you. Besides, what am I supposed to tell Mrs. White?"

We argued for a while, and I said I'd sleep on it. The next morning, I relented and said I'd give Mary a call.

Besides being former neighbors, Mary and I were in the same first grade class, where she was a friendly face and trusted companion. My only memory of her from those days is walking around the playground together one day during recess. For no apparent reason, our classmate Jimmy Fitzgerald confronted us and started giving us a hard time.

"Tommy loves Maa-ry! Tommy loves Maa-ry!"

"Cut it out, Jimmy!" I said.

Then he got right up in our faces and started singing, "Tommy and Mary, sittin' in a tree, K-I-S-S-I-N-G," which he followed up with some loud, obnoxious laughter.

Wanting him to stop, I pushed him away, and he pushed me back. More pushing and shoving followed, and this attracted the attention of the other kids, who gathered around us to see what would come of the conflict. Suddenly, Miss Comer, our teacher, appeared out of nowhere to grab Jimmy and me and pull us apart. Then the bell rang, and we all headed back inside. Miss Comer was still holding on to us, and she told us to stand beside her desk at the front of the class while she conducted an investigation.

The other kids are all sitting in their places, waiting for the drama to unfold. I'm just standing there, feeling scared and embarrassed, worried about what my parents will think when they find out.

"So who started the pushing match?" Miss Comer asks as she eyes the two of us.

Jimmy and I are both looking down at the floor, shuffling our feet, unable to speak.

"Thomas...James...I'd like to know who started it."

As we continue to remain silent, one of my friends in the class raises his hand and says, "I saw the whole thing, Miss Comer."

"OK, Arthur, what did you see?"

"Well, Tommy was just walking around the playground with Mary, minding his own business, when Jimmy walked up to them and started pushing him."

"That's right," I say.

Miss Comer then looks at Jimmy and asks, "Is this true, James?"

Instead of saying something in his own defense, Jimmy starts sobbing. Miss Comer lets this go on for a while before delivering her verdict. "Well," she says, "in my experience the guilty party is usually the one who starts crying. So James, please dry your eyes. For your punishment, you'll have to stay inside during recess for the rest of the week."

I felt relieved, but also conflicted. I knew I was the one who started the pushing. I also knew Jimmy was a troublemaker who wasn't well-liked by the other kids or our teacher, while I was well-behaved and had some loyal friends in the class. What I didn't know is whether Artie lied to protect me, or if he really thought Jimmy pushed me first. I felt sorry for Jimmy, and guilty that I corroborated Artie's story, but not sorry or guilty enough to say anything. I was too afraid of getting in trouble and disappointing Miss Comer, not to mention my parents.

Getting back to Mary, after first grade, we ended up in different social and academic circles, especially in high school, and we pretty much lost track of each other. So when I called to ask if she'd like to go to the prom with me, it felt strange. But after she said yes, as expected, we continued to chat and decided to go out once or twice before the prom to get reacquainted. I asked her if she'd like to see *Ryan's Daughter*, a romantic epic set on the Irish coast during World War I, at our local cinema. She said she'd love to.

After the movie, we stopped to get ice cream and talk about the film, to which we gave mixed reviews. Then it was time to take her home. I wasn't especially drawn to Mary, but I could see she was an attractive young woman, and I knew she was a good person, too. Despite my initial resistance to calling her, I was grateful we'd be going to the prom together and sharing this rite of passage.

The windows of my father's car were rolled down as I pulled into the White's driveway. The air was balmy, the moon was shining brightly, the crickets were chirping lustily, and the scent of apple blossoms was in the air. I told Mary I had a good time, which was true. She smiled and said she had a good time, too. Then I leaned over for a goodnight kiss, and when our lips met, I suddenly, unexpectedly found her tongue inside my mouth. Although this surprised me, I was even more surprised to discover I knew exactly what to do with it, and I was overwhelmed by the instantaneous reactions in my body: the pounding of my heart, the stirring in my groin, the desire for this kiss to go on and on. After a minute or so, we stopped. Mary opened the car door, thanked me for the movie and the ride home, smiled once again, and said good night. As I watched her disappear into her parents' house, I backed out of the driveway and headed for home, aware that something new and powerful was stirring inside me. What I didn't realize was that something else had been lost forever, and that there would never be another kiss quite as memorable as this first one again.

Mary and I went to the prom with another couple – my friend Paul Cicco (the twin brother of my friend Peter from the Israelites) and his girlfriend Karen. When the big night arrived, we dressed up in our tuxedos and floor-length gowns and posed for pictures in my parents' living room. Later, when the formal dinner/dance and the after-party wrapped up, I drove the four of us to a beach in Gloucester, where we sat, held each other, smooched a little, and waited for the sun to come up. I was so exhausted and disoriented during the drive home that when we got to a familiar intersection near Karen's house, I had to wake up Paul, who was asleep in the front seat beside me, because I couldn't remember which way to turn.

The following week, Mary and I talked things over and decided not to pursue our relationship any further. She was going off to nursing school somewhere out West, while I was staying close to home. That summer, I had a brief fling with a flute player from the high school band, but when the star quarterback from our football team gave her a call, she decided she'd rather go out with him. At that point, all I could do was look forward to going away to college and putting Chelmsford behind me.

CHAPTER SEVEN

College Bound

Thanks to my parents' ability to drop subtle and sometimes not-so-subtle hints to let me know what was expected of me, I had a clear goal throughout my high school years: getting the best grades I possibly could. Eventually, that goal became getting into the best college I possibly could. So when the fat envelope from Harvard showed up in our mailbox one Saturday morning in April of 1971, I was thrilled beyond words. With my smiling parents looking on, I literally jumped up and down for joy. We had hit the jackpot. Now all I had to do was cash in the chips. Or so I thought.

When I arrived on campus the following September, I was riding high. But the joy didn't last long. I looked around and saw that my classmates were an impressive bunch. Many were already planning to go to medical, law, or business school after college, and they knew they wanted to major in biology, government, or economics. I, however, had no idea what I wanted to do when I grew up. So when I had to declare a major toward the end of freshman year, I was stumped.

After toying with the idea of majoring in music or going pre-med (which would have thrilled my parents), I chose to major in English. I didn't know where that might lead, but I liked to read and write, and I figured that studying the great works of English and American literature would be a fine way to spend my undergraduate years.

Of course, academics weren't the only thing on my mind. I was living away from home for the first time, the sexual revolution was in full swing, and my hormones were urging me to join the cause. But I was still self-conscious and shy around women, especially the ones I was attracted to. I wasn't helped by the fact that the ratio of men to women on campus at the time was something like 4:1. And as a freshman, I was assigned to live in Harvard Yard, which at the time was the last all-male enclave on campus. So in order to meet eligible females, I'd tag along with other frustrated freshman guys to Friday night mixers at local women's colleges, but I could never work up the courage to ask someone to dance.

I also visited my family regularly, usually by driving out to Chelmsford with Nonno and Nonna Sica for Sunday dinner. On one of those Sundays halfway through the school year, with the family gathered around the dining room table, my mother told me about a distant relative she'd met the night before at a wedding.

"Her name is Anita, and I really liked her," she said enthusiastically.

"That's nice, Mom," was my nonchalant reply.

"We talked for a while, and she told me she's a sophomore at Regis College in Weston."

"Uh-huh," I muttered as I took a sip from my wine glass.

"I told her you're a freshman at Harvard."

"Uh-huh," I repeated, with a rising sense of dread.

"She said she'd like to meet you, so I asked for her phone number."

"Oh, Mom," I whined, "what did you do that for?"

"What did I do? She's your cousin. I thought you might like to meet her."

"Sounds like a set-up to me."

"Don't be silly. I'll give you her number after dinner."

Mom made good on her offer, and I told her I'd call, although I had no intention of doing so.

For the next several months, whenever I saw my mother or spoke to her on the phone, she asked if I'd called Anita. And every time, I told her no, not yet. I kept hoping she'd eventually drop the idea. But I should have known better. When my mother latched on to something, she was like a hungry terrier with a bone in its mouth. She would not let it go. To put an end to the standoff, I finally gave in, called Anita, and invited her to come to Cambridge, perhaps with one of her friends, to meet me and my roommate Jeff. I didn't want to make a big deal about it. I just wanted to get it over with. Then I explained the situation to Jeff and asked if he'd be willing to hang out with me the following Saturday night and meet two women from Regis. He agreed.

Jeff and I shared a small suite of rooms on the fourth floor of Thayer Hall, an old, ivy-clad dormitory overlooking University Hall, Widener Library, and Memorial Church. The suite had two tiny bedrooms and a shared living room/study. When Anita and her friend arrived, we introduced ourselves, offered them some snacks, opened a bottle of Mateus rosé, put some records on the stereo, then sat around listening to music and talking. It wasn't nearly as awkward as I thought it would be. Anita was warm, engaging, fun to be with and, I had to admit, attractive. She had blue-gray eyes, a round and open face, a big smile, and a musical voice that was easy to listen to. After a few hours of hanging out with us, she and her friend said they had to get back to Regis and we all promised to stay in touch.

The next morning, I knew I wanted to see Anita again, and I couldn't help but wonder if it might develop into a romance. But how weird would that be? She was my cousin, after all. On the other hand, she was a distant cousin, one I never even knew existed. Doing the math, I figured she was a fourth cousin, although now that I have a better understanding of how these things work, I think she's actually a second cousin once removed. In any event, the connection was distant enough so that if we wanted to become more than just cousins, no one could raise any serious objections. In fact, my mother already seemed to be pushing the idea. Or at least that was my impression. After mulling it over, I wrote Anita a lighthearted note asking if she'd like to get together again before the school year was over. When I didn't hear back, I was surprised and disappointed, but relieved at the same time. At least I could tell my mother I followed up.

As freshman year came to an end, I felt like I was no longer the same person who arrived at Harvard the previous September. I was returning home for the summer, but I knew it wouldn't feel like home anymore. Not like it used to. Which is what I was thinking on a sunny afternoon in June as I sat on the steps of a mostly deserted Thayer Hall, waiting for my father to pick me up. So much had changed over the course of the year. I was wearing the bell-bottom blue jeans and tie-dyed t-shirt that had become the uniform of my generation. My hair was long enough to cover my ears and the back of my neck. I had smoked marijuana for the first time. I joined the protests against the war in Vietnam, and one night in Harvard Square that spring I inhaled the pungent aroma of tear gas.

By no stretch of the imagination was I a radical extremist, but I was way left of center, was opposed to the military-industrial complex, and was hoping the United States could become a nation that valued peace and justice more than conquest, exploitation, and profits. Inspired by *The Greening of America,* I read other books that were critical of our capitalist, materialistic culture, and that hinted at more vital and meaningful alternatives: Jack Kerouac's *Dharma Bums,* Norman Mailer's *Armies of the Night,* Tom Wolfe's *The Electric Kool-Aid Acid Test,* and Ken Kesey's *One Flew Over the Cuckoo's Nest,* to name just a few.

When my father pulled up in his brand new, 1972 Oldsmobile 98 Luxury Sedan, I was seeing it for the first time. It was a big car. A very big car. It was gold on the outside and gold on the inside, with a gas-guzzling V-8 engine and lots of fancy extras. After we put my boxes of books and clothes and record albums into the massive trunk, we climbed aboard, and my father started 'er up and turned on the air conditioning, which I had to admit felt good on that warm June day.

"Whaddya think?" he asked me, beaming with pride.

"Well, the AC is nice."

"You bet it is! Now watch this," he said as he pushed a button and the front seat started moving back and forth. "Power seats!"

"Wow," I said, doing my best to muster up some enthusiasm.

"And power windows, too!" he said as he pressed another button, and his window went down and back up again.

"Very cool," I replied as I tried the same thing with my window.

"I got a great deal on it and your mother is thrilled," he added. "Because it's going to be her car. I took it today because it has more trunk room than my Pontiac."

I didn't want to spoil the moment or his upbeat mood, but I was appalled. That car was a symbol of everything I was opposed to. So I changed the subject, and we chatted about other things during the ride home. One of those things was a summer job my father had heard about from a friend. I was happy to learn about this and promised to look into it.

The job was working in the mailroom and maintenance department at a chemical company in the office park where my father worked. It wasn't how I imagined spending the summer, but the pay was decent, and I'd be able to hitch a ride to and from work with my father. Since I didn't have any better offers, I took it. And for the next two and a half months, I did a variety of jobs at the firm: picking up the mail at the post office every morning, sliding all the envelopes into the appropriate slots in the mailroom, shipping and receiving barrels of chemicals at the loading dock, and doing odd jobs like painting the cafeteria and the hallways.

The high point of the summer, though, was the annual family picnic at a big park somewhere north of Boston. This event had been inaugurated a few years earlier by my maternal grandmother's family and was an attempt by the older generation to keep members of their rapidly dispersing clan in touch with each other. Paul and I had attended the previous summer's gathering and didn't enjoy it, so we wanted to skip it this time around. But my parents begged us to come, and we agreed.

When we arrived at the picnic grounds on a sizzling hot Saturday in July, we looked out upon a large, grassy expanse bordering a wooded area, with picnic tables near the trees and a baseball diamond off to one side. We also saw over a hundred of our relatives scattered about. The older folks were sitting at the picnic tables and chatting. Some of the younger relatives were playing softball, while others were firing up the charcoal grills and putting out the salads and side dishes they brought from home. Paul and I tried to make the best of it, hanging out with our grandparents, chatting with other relatives we knew, playing a little softball, helping ourselves to hamburgers and lasagna, hoping to make an early exit. But that plan changed when I spotted Anita arriving with her parents, which was a welcome surprise.

When the meal was over, I wandered over to the table where Anita and her parents were sitting. She introduced me, and then the two of us found a quiet spot under a tree where we could sit and talk. She told me she had transferred from Regis to the Boston College School of Nursing and would be starting there in the fall to complete her bachelor's degree.

"That's great," I said. "So it'll be easier for us to get together again, if you have the time and would like to, that is."

"Yes," she said, "that'd be nice."

Knowing I never got a response to the note I had sent her that spring, I wondered if I should bring this up or just let it go. I was curious, so I took a chance.

"I was actually hoping to get together with you again last spring, but I didn't hear back after I sent that note to you at Regis."

She looked at me quizzically and asked, "Note? What note?"

"Oh, I sent you a funny little note after you and your friend came over to Harvard to meet me and my roommate."

"Gee," she said, looking perplexed, "I never got it."

"Well, that's campus mail for you," I replied, feeling relieved and encouraged. "We'll have to try again in the fall."

She smiled and said, "I'd like that." And she gave me the phone number of the apartment she was renting near the BC campus.

That September, the first thing I did after settling into my new dorm room was borrow my grandparents' car and drive it out to see Anita and her new apartment. She gave me a quick tour, then we sat down and talked about our plans for the upcoming year. It was great seeing her again. And when it was time to say goodbye, my parting kiss lingered just long enough to suggest I wanted to be more than distant cousins. She seemed surprised but didn't reject the suggestion. I promised to call her again soon.

For our first date, I invited her to the Harvard football game the following Saturday. Since I was in the band, I could get her a free ticket and a seat next to me in the band section. The Harvard University Band was, and still is, an organization equally concerned with having fun as it is with making music, and she enjoyed hanging out with us, laughing at our antics, and watching the game. We quickly got to know each other that fall, and by the time November rolled around, we were very much in love. We were spending every weekend together and talking on the phone almost every night during the week. We were also introducing each other to the pleasures and joys of sexual love, which were more powerful and intoxicating than anything I had ever experienced, or even imagined, before.

Thus began what I still think of as the happiest year of my life. I couldn't believe how fortunate I was. I was in love with a wonderful woman, one who loved me just as much in return. I was a sophomore at Harvard, and I was getting good enough grades. Walking to class in the morning, I'd look at the sun shining through the trees and the shopkeepers opening their stores and the traffic flowing through Harvard Square, and I'd feel moved by how beautiful it all was. To top it off, at the annual Yale game, the final game of the football season, I was named the Harvard Band's next student conductor. I had so much to be thankful for and so much to look forward to.

Initially, my parents seemed delighted that Anita and I were a couple. But when it became obvious that we were spending so much time together, my mother started asking some pointed questions during our phone conversations.

"So the two of you went to the game on Saturday and then had breakfast together on Sunday? How did you manage that?"

"Well, she has a car, and it's a quick drive from her place to Harvard Square, especially on Sunday morning when there isn't any traffic."

This wasn't a false statement, but it was certainly a misleading one.

She called me again on another Sunday morning, and when she heard a female voice in the background, she asked, "Oh, is that Anita?"

"Yes, Mom, she stayed over last night. She was tired and we thought it was too late for her to drive home."

"So where did she sleep?"

"On the sofa in our living room."

OK, that was an outright lie. Which I felt guilty about. But I was getting sick of having to field all these intrusive questions. I finally put a stop to it one night when I was in the car with my parents, who'd been in Cambridge for some reason and stopped by to take me out to dinner. They were in the front seat, I was in the back, and they were about to drop me off at my dorm when my mother turned around and started asking more questions about Anita and me and our sleeping arrangements.

"OK, Mom," I finally said, sounding more than a little annoyed. "You want to know the truth? Anita and I are sleeping together. We've been sleeping together since sometime back in October. We're in love, and we're very happy together. And we're being careful because we're not stupid, OK?"

She gasped and started to state her objections, but my father, in an uncharacteristically assertive move, interrupted her.

"Marianne," he said. "That's enough."

She stopped midsentence. I opened the back door, thanked them for dinner, and got out of the car. The subject was never brought up again.

On a Saturday morning that spring, I was lying in bed with Anita, holding her in my arms in post-coital bliss, thinking that it just doesn't get any better than this, that I had found the woman I was destined to spend the rest of my life with. Then I suddenly sat up, looked her in the eyes and blurted out, "Will you marry me?" Without hesitating, she laughed and said, "Yes!"

For the rest of the weekend we were giddy with excitement. But after she went back to her apartment on Sunday afternoon, reality set in, at least for me. My mind was filled with doubts and second thoughts. "What have I done?" I asked myself. "Am I really ready for this? I'm only nineteen years old!"

I knew Anita was clear about wanting a career in nursing, and I suspected she wanted to have children, too. But I still didn't know what I wanted to do with my life. As the week wore on, the doubts and the questions wore me down, and I knew I had to say something to her. Which wasn't easy. In fact, I felt like a real jerk when I brought it up the following weekend.

"I'm so sorry," I said. "I should've thought things through a lot more before asking you something like that. But I think it's too soon for us to make that kind of decision." To her credit, she said she understood, and assured me that we had plenty of time to figure things out after we both graduated.

When sophomore year ended, I moved back in with my family and had the same summer job. Anita was with her family at their summer home in Nahant. We continued to get together every weekend, and although spending the night together was no longer feasible, we didn't mind. Our commitment to each other remained strong. In September, we went back to school, and things picked up pretty much where we'd left them in the spring. Another football season began, and Anita was by my side at every home game. Plus, now that I was student conductor, I was directing the music on the field at halftime, in the stands during the game, and at a postgame serenade for the team at their field house. It was a heady experience, and I was feeling good about myself. Maybe a little too good.

Things began to change during that 1973 football season. Before then, very few women were in the band. In fact, it was an all-male organization from the time it was founded in 1919 until women were finally allowed to join in 1970. At first, only a few brave females dared to do so. But the fall of 1973 brought a significant influx of young women, mostly from that year's freshman class. One of them was a clarinetist who enjoyed hanging around the band room and being "one of the guys." Pat was clever, funny, and had an outgoing personality. Several upper classmen were interested in getting to know her better, and much to my surprise, I became one of them. I wasn't planning to do anything about it until I began to suspect that she might be interested in me. She liked to kid around with me and was always friendly in an inviting kind of way. At least that's how I perceived it. Sometimes when I was conducting and our eyes met, she'd pull her clarinet away from her lips, smile, and mouth the word, "Pompous," which was the rather inappropriate nickname I was given after Harvard trounced the UMass football team and a reporter from the UMass *Daily Collegian* wrote a sour-grapes article about the game. He mocked everything Harvardian as elitist and effete, including the fancy tailgate parties, the ivy-covered stadium, and "the pompous conductor who led the band in a series of Harvard fight songs from the roof of their field house after the game." When someone tacked a copy of that article to the bulletin board in the band room the following week, I immediately became "Pompous" to everyone in and around with the band.

Watching this attractive young freshman whisper that name in a clandestine yet public way was titillating and irresistible. Was she encouraging me to pursue her? I didn't know, but that's exactly what it made me want to do. I thought about what it would be like to be with her, and the more I thought about it, the more my feelings for Anita faded. But what was I to do? I couldn't bring myself to talk about it with anyone, especially not Anita. And I didn't want to sneak around behind her back. I eventually concluded that I wasn't in love with her anymore, that what we had wasn't "true love," and that I had to let her go. One night, I finally worked up the courage to tell her. She was surprised and hurt, and she begged me to reconsider. But my mind was made up. Even when I realized a month or so later that the young clarinetist I'd fallen so hard for would never feel the same way about me, I didn't go running back to Anita. Maybe I was too proud, or too immature, or too afraid she'd refuse to take me back. All I knew was that I had let her go, and I needed to move on.

CHAPTER EIGHT

Now What?

Toward the end of my junior year I became friendly with a French horn player in the band, and we kept in touch by mail over the summer. I sensed she was interested in a deeper relationship, and I was open to the idea. Janet was unlike anyone I'd been involved with before. For one thing, she was Jewish. And with her New Jersey accent, she combined a tomboyish toughness with a self-deprecating sense of humor I found appealing. When we returned to Cambridge in the fall, we started dating, and the chemistry between us felt strong. I wasn't in love with her, but I genuinely liked her and was intrigued by her offbeat personality. I thought that perhaps, in time, love might grow. But when we ended up in bed together for the first time, things didn't go so well. I couldn't consummate our relationship, which was a surprise to me as well as a major embarrassment. Janet was cool about it and didn't say or do anything to make me feel any worse than I already did. We tried a couple more times over the next few weeks, with no improvement. I decided it was probably because I wasn't in love with her and didn't want to end up hurting her the way I'd hurt Anita. When I said I wanted to go back to being just friends, she didn't seem surprised or upset. We remained friends and stayed in touch, at least until she married a man from England a few years after she graduated from Harvard.

Since I was a senior, I decided to forget about relationships for a while and try to figure out what I wanted to do when I got my diploma. After four years of college, I still didn't have a clue. My parents' influence over me had waned as I made my way through college, and as they became more focused on my two youngest siblings: eleven-year-old Pete and eight-year-old Maryellen. So it was all up to me now, and the big question was still, *What the hell do I want to do with the rest of my goddamn life?* The answer was far from clear. Applying to law, medical or business school held no appeal. Taking a year off to travel, see the world, and somehow "find myself" felt like a waste of time. And I didn't want to settle for any old job just to make money. After embracing the values of the '60s counterculture, I wanted to pursue something I could believe in. Something that would make a difference in the world. Since I was an English major, I decided that teaching high school English might help me do just that. I imagined myself in front of a classroom of eager learners, molding young minds and inspiring the next generation. That felt like a good way to spend at least a few years, and maybe the rest of my life.

So one week after graduation, I headed west to start the Master of Arts in Teaching program at Northwestern University. I applied to that program because it was short – just 15 months – and because it virtually paid for itself. As an MAT student, I'd take classes all summer at Northwestern, then work as a teaching intern during the academic year at a local high school, where I'd earn a part-time teacher's salary that would cover my tuition and most of my living expenses. Then I'd finish up the following summer with more classes at Northwestern. This meant I could get my degree and teacher certification without needing a student loan or asking my parents to continue subsidizing my education.

At first, I was thrilled with the program. There was a camaraderie among my fellow students that was very different from the competitive atmosphere at Harvard, and I loved being part of it. I also made a connection with one of my professors, a charismatic guy with a bushy beard and a look of determination in his eyes. Marty Nystrand was committed to improving the quality of education in the United States, and he inspired me to take my decision to become a teacher more seriously. He helped me see that in addition to educating young people, teaching can be a way to have a positive impact on society as a whole. That first summer, I was a student teacher under a veteran English teacher at Evanston High School, and I watched him motivate his students to work harder and do better. I was impressed, and I believed I was laying the groundwork for a rewarding career.

But everything changed in the fall, when I became a teaching intern at New Trier North High School in Winnetka. As an intern, I'd be teaching two classes of sophomore English and one of freshman English. This time, it would be just me and the kids, with no senior teacher in sight. I remember sitting in the teachers' room the week before classes began when one of the older teachers asked to see the rosters of my three classes. After looking them over he let out a low whistle and said, "Wow, you've got some big challenges here."

He knew what he was talking about. New Trier North served an upper middle-class community, and many of its graduates got into elite colleges. But most of the kids I was assigned to teach were academically challenged. Some had learning disabilities. Others came from troubled families and were carrying emotional and psychological wounds. Almost all had low self-esteem and no interest in learning how to diagram a sentence or analyze a poem. On the first day of school, feeling the dampness in my armpits and the tightness in my gut as I walked down the long hallway toward my first class, I heard a loud crash from inside the room. When I walked in, I saw an overturned desk and two boys engaged in a wrestling match. They stopped when they realized I had arrived, and all eyes turned to me, the new teacher who hadn't even introduced himself yet.

"What's going on here?" I asked, trying to sound as stern as possible.

"Danny called me an asshole!" one of them said.

"He called me a fag!" said the other.

What was I supposed to do? Send them both to the principal's office? That probably would have been an excellent idea. But since no real harm was done, and because I was reluctant to take such a drastic step, I just scowled at them, shook my head in disgust, and told them to put the desk back and take their seats. Which they did. But I was already losing control of the class. As the weeks and months dragged on, that became obvious, especially in my two sophomore classes. While I tried to focus the kids' attention on the lesson of the day, I was regularly interrupted by boys throwing spitballs and girls passing notes or having side conversations about the boys. At night I'd lie in bed exhausted, staring at the ceiling, unable to sleep, dreading what the next day would bring.

My training up to that point emphasized "student-centered teaching," without any tips on how to establish and maintain classroom discipline. And I definitely needed help in that department. On the phone with my parents one night, as I complained about the chaos in my classrooms, my father told me to put my foot down, and "not be a Caspar Milquetoast." That was an expression he liked to use. It was his way of saying "C'mon, buck up and be a man." But it made me feel even worse, because I believed I'd already become Mr. Milquetoast, a pushover, a pitiful failure, and I didn't think there was anything I could do about it. Or, when I was feeling a little kinder toward myself, I thought that maybe I just wasn't cut out to be a high school teacher, and that I should try something else. Somehow, I muddled through until the semester ended, but by that time I'd dropped out of the MAT program and submitted a resignation letter to my department head at New Trier.

Feeling defeated, I packed my bags and prepared to return to Massachusetts. The night before I left, my fellow MAT students threw a farewell party for me, which delighted me because it showed they cared and saddened me because I knew I'd probably never see any of them again. Early the next day, on a cold, clear December morning, I got into my car and started the engine. Then I turned on the radio and heard strange, staticky voices interfering with the local station I was expecting to hear. Out of curiosity, I fiddled with the dial, hoping to pick up this rogue signal, and I eventually did. When I heard the announcer say it was WBZ in Boston, I was amazed. "I don't believe this!" I said out loud, to no one in particular. I knew 'BZ had a powerful signal, but I never imagined it could reach the suburbs of Chicago. As I pulled out of my parking space and headed east into the sun that was peeking over the horizon, WBZ faded away. But I saw its appearance as a sign I was heading in the right direction.

Two days later, I was back in my parents' house in Chelmsford. It was humbling. They were happy I was home again, and although they didn't say it, I'm sure they were relieved I decided to drop the idea of becoming a high school teacher. They still had bigger dreams for their Harvard-educated son.

But after my experience at New Trier North, I was shaken. I was also ready to put aside any thoughts I had about helping other people and making the world a better place. I just wanted to get a job and make some money.

At that point, my simple goal was finding work as soon as possible and getting on with my life. Unfortunately, that wasn't as easy as I thought it would be. The post-Vietnam War economy was in recession, and job prospects for recent college grads were poor. I also lacked any marketable skills. I had always enjoyed writing, however, and had been vaguely interested in advertising since the mid-'60s, when the "creative revolution" on Madison Avenue spawned a series of clever, irreverent ad campaigns for companies like Volkswagen, Avis, and Alka-Seltzer. So I thought maybe, just maybe, I could become one of the copywriters who create such memorable, entertaining ads.

I focused my efforts on finding a job in the advertising business, with publishing as a second choice. Eventually, I was able to schedule informational interviews with people in both fields, and I was told the ad biz would be tougher to break into, partly because of the recession, and partly because I'd have to put together a portfolio of speculative ads to demonstrate my copywriting skills to the creative directors who had the power to hire me. Undeterred, I started working on my spec portfolio. But I also continued looking for openings at publishing companies.

One of those publishers – Addison Wesley in Reading, Massachusetts – was launching a new training program for college textbook sales reps, and I was being considered for one of three places in that program. At the same time, I was showing my newly created portfolio to local ad agencies, and got a positive response from Brian Turley, the creative director at a Boston agency called The DR Group. Although he liked my work, Brian didn't have any openings. But he asked me to keep in touch. Not long after that, I got an offer to work for Addison Wesley. I was still more interested in creating ads than selling textbooks, but after four months of job hunting, the balance in my checking account was close to zero, I hadn't received any offers to work as a copywriter, and I had a pretty good one in hand from Addison Wesley. Before I accepted it, though, I wrote a last-ditch letter to Brian that began, "I am about to offer you a rare and wonderful opportunity: The chance to save a life."

The letter went on to say I was about to take a job as a college textbook sales rep, even though I believed I'd be much happier and more successful as an advertising copywriter. It also claimed that he could save me from a life of quiet desperation by offering me a job now, before it was too late. He called and said he loved my letter and would like to hire me, but the agency's fiscally conservative chairman told him they just didn't have the money bring in a new writer.

So I went to work for Addison Wesley and tried to make the best of it. After five months of in-house training, I was given a company car and the choice of three territories: Atlanta, Chicago, or Nashville. Since I knew people in the Chicago area, I packed up my car and headed west.

After renting a studio apartment and reconnecting with friends from Northwestern, I went to work. Despite the extensive training, however, I wasn't prepared for the life of a traveling sales rep. The nearest Addison Wesley employee was my sales manager, who lived in Indiana and called once a week to check in. All by myself, I was expected to visit all the colleges in northern Illinois, decide which AW textbooks were appropriate for the various courses each college was offering, drop off samples of those books to the professors who were teaching those courses, and follow up with phone calls or in-person visits to encourage the professors to look at, comment on, and ultimately adopt our books for their courses. It was lonely work with virtually no feedback of any kind. There was no one to pat me on the back and tell me I was doing a good job or perhaps point out ways I could improve. I wouldn't even know if I made any sales until the end of the semester, or in some cases, until the end of the academic year.

On a rainy Friday night in late September I was feeling discouraged. But I was determined not to disappoint the people who hired me back at AW corporate headquarters. As I prepared a dinner of Hamburger Helper in my apartment and tried to ignore the loud music coming from next door, the phone rang. Hoping it was a friend from Northwestern calling to make plans for the weekend, I picked it up and said hello.

"You're a tough guy to track down," the voice at the other end of the line said. "I had to call your parents in Chelmsford, who gave me your number in Chicago. And this is the third time I've called this week. Don't you have an answering machine?"

"Uh, no, not yet. I'm still getting settled. And who's this?"

"It's Brian Turley from The DR Group in Boston. Remember me?"

"Brian! Of course, I remember you. How are things at The DR Group?"

"Well, things have changed. You know I really wanted to hire you last spring because I liked your portfolio, and that last letter you sent me was fabulous. But there just wasn't any room in the budget."

"Yes, I know."

"Well, we've landed a new account, and the chairman gave me the go-ahead to hire another writer. So I'm offering you the job."

I couldn't believe what I was hearing. Why hadn't this happened eight months ago? Of course, I was flattered. And I was tempted. But I immediately thought of Steve, the guy at AW who hired the other two trainees and me and who had high hopes for all of us, especially since this new training program was designed to cut down on the high turnover rate among first-year sales reps. And I couldn't imagine telling him I was quitting after just a month in the field.

"Really? Well, gee, Brian, I don't know. I'd like to say yes. But Addison Wesley just put me through a five-month training program and is expecting me to start selling books for them. They'd be really upset if I quit now."

"Yeah, I understand. The timing isn't great. Look, why don't you think about it over the weekend and call me back on Monday."

"OK, I can do that. And thanks for remembering me."

That was how one of the most stressful weekends of my life began. I was excited about the offer from Brian, but I felt guilty about disappointing Steve and the folks at Addison Wesley. After my first month in the field, I wasn't looking forward to selling textbooks all over Chicagoland for the next few years. On the other hand, the job was fairly secure, and I didn't know if I could make it as a copywriter in the cutthroat, competitive world of advertising. Plus, moving back to my old bedroom in Chelmsford from Chicago for the second time in less than a year would be humiliating. I called my parents, who said they'd love to have me back in the Boston area but would understand if I decided to stay in Chicago. I called friends, who all agreed it was a tough decision. I hemmed and hawed, deliberated, ruminated, made lists of pros and cons. But I couldn't make up my mind. Finally, on Sunday afternoon, I took a ride to the town of Wilmette, just north of Chicago, to visit Lotte Steinfeld.

Lotte was in her mid-seventies, and she lived with her younger sister, Ruth Friedman. The two fled Nazi Germany in the 1930s to avoid the horrors that were beginning to unfold there. I never asked what happened to the rest of their family. All I knew was that the two of them were living in this big Victorian house, and in order to defray the cost of maintaining the place, they rented out rooms to male grad students from Northwestern.

"We only take graduate students," Lotte told me when I answered the ad she'd posted at Northwestern the previous year, "because they're quieter and more mature than undergraduates. And we only take men because, well, Ruth and I think it's a good idea to have some men in the house."

I became one of those men while I was in Northwestern's MAT program. And during the short time I lived in her house, I grew fond of Lotte. In fact, to show my appreciation before I moved out, I took the apparently unprecedented step of inviting her and Ruth to dinner in the makeshift basement kitchen I shared with the other male grad students. Both women said they were touched by my gesture, if not by my cooking.

Lotte didn't know I was back in the area. But as I continued to struggle with my decision, something told me this might be a good time to return to the house in Wilmette and check in with her. Maybe she could help me figure out what to do without pushing me one way or the other. So I called and invited myself over.

"Come in, Thomas, come in," she said in her lilting German accent as she opened the door.

Her steel-gray hair was neatly tied back, as usual, in a bun. And her piercing blue eyes beamed at me through her rimless glasses. Lotte was an intelligent and sensitive woman, but shrewd and tough at the same time. Those eyes had seen a lot. They helped her survive the rise of Fascism in Germany, not to mention the challenges of emigrating to the U.S. during the Great Depression and starting over.

"I'll make us a pot of tea and you can tell me what you've been up to."

I followed her into the kitchen and smelled the chocolate chip cookies she had just finished baking. A vase of yellow mums adorned the table. She poured us some tea and I told her my tale. I described my lengthy job search. My dueling interests in advertising and publishing. My training program at Addison Wesley. My return to Chicago to sell textbooks. My Friday night call from Boston with an offer to join an ad agency as a copywriter. My reluctance to disappoint my boss at the publishing company. My fears about moving back to Boston to start a new job with an uncertain future.

"Mrs. Steinfeld, I don't know what to do," I finally said as I shook my head and sighed. "And I don't know how I'm going to decide."

She took a sip of tea and looked at me with those intelligent, sensitive eyes. "Thomas," she said. "I think you already have."

At first, I didn't know what she meant. But then I thought back to how my voice sounded when I described my two options to her – disappointed when I talked about sticking with Addison Wesley, excited when I talked about joining The DR Group. And I realized that this was what she heard – not the words I used, but the feelings behind them.

"I want to take the job in Boston, don't I?"

"That's right."

And just like that, my mind was made up. I sat back, chuckled to myself, smiled at Lotte and said, "I'm glad we had this talk."

It was a brief conversation, but Lotte's ability to listen with an open mind, an open heart, and without an agenda of her own made it a profound one. I don't think anyone had ever listened to me like that before. And it was a revelation. It was as if I suddenly woke up from a trance, got out of my head and into my heart, and knew what I wanted to do.

I wanted to work in advertising.

CHAPTER NINE

Becoming a Mad Man

My first day as a copywriter began on an October morning in 1976 when I arrived at The DR Group's office in downtown Boston just before nine. Wearing a brand-new suit and feeling nervous, I introduced myself to the receptionist and took a seat in the small lobby. A few minutes later, I was greeted by my new boss, Brian Turley, a burly Irish American twice my size and twenty years my senior. He was also wearing a much nicer suit.

Brian ushered me into his office, which featured a colorful Persian rug, a pair of Queen Anne guest chairs and a mahogany desk. He gestured for me to sit in one of the guest chairs as he took a seat behind the desk. After some small talk, he told me about the accounts I'd be working on. The list included Western Union, Pitney Bowes and the *Wall Street Journal*, and since these were all big blue-chip companies, this was both exciting and intimidating to hear. Then he took me on a tour of the office and introduced me to some of the 25 or so people who worked there. Like Ray Smith, a portly production manager with a handlebar mustache who, in his spare time, played drums in a Dixieland band and hosted "The Jazz Decades," a weekly show on WGBH radio. And Carroll Johnson, a thin, elderly, frail-looking copywriter with tobacco-stained fingers whose desk was surrounded by about a dozen *Playboy* centerfolds he had tacked up on the walls of his cubicle. After the tour, Brian dropped me off at my own cubicle, which was down the hall from Carroll's at the end of long row of cubicles, and as I listened to the sounds of telephones ringing, typewriters click-clacking, and people chattering, I started to worry that with all this racket, how would I ever be able to concentrate long enough to write anything good?

After a few minutes, I heard Carroll strolling by my cubicle, sipping on his first coffee of the morning, slowly making his way down the hall. Then he stopped, sighed heavily, and said, just loud enough for all of us cubicle dwellers to hear, "Will the day never end?"

But the most surprising part of that first day was lunch.

When he left me at my cubicle, Brian said he'd be back at noon to take me to lunch. Obviously, he was going out of his way to welcome me and make me feel like part of his team. As I worked my way through a folder filled with health insurance forms and other orientation materials, I imagined us going to Locke-Ober or one of the other fine restaurants in downtown Boston at the time. So I was surprised when, at the appointed hour, he led me across the street to an establishment called The Blue Sands.

Although I'd never heard of it, I soon discovered that The Blue Sands was your classic dive bar. As we entered and my eyes adjusted to the dim light, I saw that one side of the long, windowless room featured the bar itself, where a number of down-and-out looking older men sat nursing their drinks. Along the other side was a series of booths. Brian led me to one of them, which I'd later learn was "his" booth, and we sat down. He asked me how things were going, but before I could answer, we were interrupted by a tough-looking older woman who wore a white apron and had a deep, gravelly voice.

"Hi, Brian," she said as she put a 16-ounce bottle of Narragansett beer and a big, frosted mug down in front of him.

"Tom, this is Doris," said Brian. "Doris, this is Tom, our new writer. Today's his first day."

"Hi there, hon. What'll you have?"

"Umm, I'll take a Budweiser draft," I said, even though I didn't feel like having a beer.

Doris soon returned with my draft and a second 16-ounce 'Gansett for Brian. He and I continued chatting, and after a while we were joined by Steve Tharler, who asked me to slide over as he took a seat next to me. Steve had been working at DR for six years and, as the agency's copy chief, was my immediate supervisor. When Doris came back with a third 'Gansett for Brian, Steve ordered a Coke and a cheeseburger. He also told me that if I wanted to eat, I'd better order something. So I ordered a cheeseburger, too. When we finished our burgers half an hour later, Steve turned to me and said, "OK, let's go." Then the two of us paid Doris our share of the tab, left Brian with his latest 'Gansett, and started walking back to the office.

Confused about what had just gone down, I hesitated, but finally asked, "Doesn't Brian eat?"

Steve chuckled and said, "Well, given his size, we assume he must eat at some point. But no one's ever seen him actually do it."

He then went on to explain that when Brian was promoted to creative director a few years earlier, he negotiated for the right to take a two-hour lunch break, which he almost always spends in his booth at The Sands.

This strange new world was a lot less regimented and restrained than what I'd experienced at New Trier North High School and Addison Wesley Publishing Company. I wasn't sure what to make of it, but I was intrigued.

From day one, however, I saw The DR Group as a temporary stop. Why? Because it was an agency that specialized in direct mail. So for as long as I worked there, I'd never have a chance to do what I'd been fantasizing about since I started seeking a job in advertising: writing the kind of print ads and TV commercials that get talked about around water coolers and win awards for creativity.

Still, DR was a good place to learn the craft of copywriting, discover if I had the right stuff, and get experience working on major national accounts. I also found out what it was like working with a creative director, art directors, account executives, production managers and all the other folks who make up the staff of an ad agency. As a side benefit, quite a few of those folks were, like me, in their twenties and single. We naturally gravitated toward each other, sometimes going out to lunch together or gathering for drinks at one of the local pubs (not The Blue Sands) after work on Friday. The DR Group became the center of my social as well as my professional life, especially after I moved out of my parents' house and into an apartment in Malden, just a short subway ride from downtown Boston.

I soon found myself attracted to one of the other DR twenty-somethings, a production assistant who lived with her parents in Weymouth, a middle-class town not unlike Chelmsford, but on the south side of Boston. We went out a few times and seemed to have much in common, but she made it clear she wasn't interested in a romantic relationship, which was disappointing. After my break-up with Anita and my aborted relationship with Janet, I was feeling lonely and needy, and I desperately wanted a girlfriend. Since I was too shy to approach the women I'd see at the local pubs, I signed up with a dating service, which led to a few awkward first dates, but nothing more.

Around that time, Brian Turley hired a new assistant. Heather was blond, beautiful, and moved with the grace of a dancer. She was also an extrovert, and in addition to her administrative duties, she took on the unpaid position of social director for all the company twenty-somethings. Unlike the rest of us, she had no interest in launching a career in advertising. She just wanted to have fun.

Soon, those after-hours gatherings at local watering holes were becoming more frequent, along with house parties on the weekends and outings to places like Fenway Park and Block Island. These events usually included the consumption of alcohol, and although I wasn't much of a drinker, as a shy guy I appreciated the disinhibiting effects a drink or two can have.

Heather also liked to socialize in the office. When she didn't have anything else to do, she'd stroll down the hall past all the cubicles and drop in on folks to chat. I always looked forward to her visits, partly because I liked just looking at her, but also because she had a great sense of humor, and I knew our time together would be punctuated with laughs. As these visits continued, she got into the playful habit of greeting me with, "Hi, cutie," to which I got into the playful habit of responding with, "Hi, sweetie." Sometimes we'd also grab a quick lunch together or, since we were both into running, go for a run together after work.

All this would have been extremely encouraging, if not for one unfortunate fact: Heather was married. She and her husband Joe recently moved to Massachusetts so he could attend Suffolk Law School. Since he was preoccupied with his studies and neither he nor Heather had friends or family in the area, she had some free time to fill. We never talked much about Joe, but I met him at a few of the social events Heather helped organize, and he seemed like a nice guy. Everyone thought they were a great couple and assumed they were happy together. But as I got to know Heather better, I realized she was feeling lonely and neglected. Just like me. And soon, I found myself fantasizing about rescuing her from an unhappy marriage and building a new life together.

Our relationship took a dramatic turn one night when one of The DR Group's suppliers, a printing company, invited a bunch of us to their facility after hours so they could show off their latest capabilities. When the presentation ended, there was a cocktail hour, and Heather and I both drank more than we should have. Since she lived in Medford, which was on the way to my apartment in Malden, we shared a cab ride home. And a few minutes after we told the driver where to take us, we started making out in the back seat like two love-starved teenagers. When the cab pulled up in front of her house, I had to let her go, but I knew our relationship had taken an exciting and scandalous turn. After that, our flirting continued to escalate, and I continued to suppress any feelings of shame or guilt, as well as any sense of propriety.

A month or so later, after having dinner and sharing a few too many drinks at a jazz club in Cambridge, Heather and I go back to my place, and I can barely contain my excitement.

The moment we step inside my apartment and the door clicks shut behind us, we start kissing passionately. We let our coats drop to the floor. We press our bodies together and allow our hands to roam. After a few minutes, we move into my bedroom, where we continue the kissing and the groping and the removal of clothing. Then we rip off the bedspread and, just as we're about to lie down together and bring the scene to its much-anticipated climax, the phone next to my bed starts to ring. We stop and look at each other.

"Don't answer it," she whispers. "It might be Joe."

The phone rings and rings and rings. I'm wondering if she told Joe we were going out for dinner together, but I'm afraid to ask. After about twenty rings, it finally stops. The atmosphere in the room has changed, and we hesitate for a moment or two. But we've gone this far and neither one of us is going to turn back now. Well, at least I'm not. My desire for Heather is overpowering. We start kissing again. Then Heather lies down on the bed and holds her hand out to me. I take her hand, lie next to her, and as we prepare to consummate our relationship, much to my surprise and horror, without wanting to, without meaning to, and with no warning whatsoever, I spill my seed onto the bedsheet beneath us. It's an ejaculation, for sure, but with no orgasm involved for either of us, it's the ultimate anti-climactic moment. Disappointment doesn't begin to describe how I feel about this rude interruption to our heated affair. I feel ashamed, confused, devastated. I want to disappear. But there's nowhere to run, nowhere to hide. And I don't know what to do. Finally, I say, "I'm so sorry. I don't know what happened..."

Heather looks at me and sighs. She says, "It's OK, but I think you'd better take me home now." She gets up and starts putting her clothes back on. I look at the clock and see it's after midnight. I get dressed, too. Then we get in my car and take a ride on the quiet, mostly deserted streets. After ten minutes of awkward silence, we reach her house, and because the lights are still on, Heather asks me to drop her off at the nearest corner instead of in her driveway, which sounds like a good idea.

When I get back to my apartment, I flop down on the bed and want to cry. But I can't. I also can't sleep. The same question keeps looping through my mind: What's wrong with me? What's wrong with me? What's wrong with me?

It was a painful but intriguing question. The same sexual misfiring had occurred when Janet and I tried to make love during my senior year in college. But that was different, and I could rationalize why it happened. I wasn't in love with Janet, but I suspected she was falling in love with me. So I was afraid that if we had the kind of intense sexual experiences I shared with Anita, then she'd definitely fall in love with me, and I'd end up hurting her. Badly. Just like I hurt Anita. And I didn't want to do that. So when things with Janet didn't go well in the bedroom, I was disappointed but also relieved. It gave me an excuse to end our romance before things got too complicated.

But I *was* in love with Heather. At least I believed I was. And I didn't care if she was married. I still wanted her, desperately, and I wanted to feel what it would be like to make mad, passionate love with her. To make her a part of my life. I suppose I also wanted to prove something to her and, perhaps even more so, to myself. Of course, we continued to see each other every day at the office, and the attraction between us remained strong. We soon found ourselves back in my bedroom a few more times, always with the same disappointing result. And each time it happened, I sank lower and lower into a state of self-loathing and despair. Finally, out of sheer frustration, I said I thought we should go back to being just friends. But I continued to wallow in shame and self-pity. In fact, I can say now that I've never felt so depressed and alone in my entire life.

Looking back on it, I can see that while I may have been in love with Heather, and even though this was the late '70s, a time when it seemed like everyone was sleeping with everyone else, my inner altar boy just wouldn't let me get in on the fun. In fact, he had a point. After all, Heather was *married*. And I'd been subjected to a lot of conditioning about marriage being sacred and sex being sinful unless it took place within the bonds of holy matrimony. Apparently, part of me still believed that. But another part yearned to be free of those old-fashioned, puritanical, bourgeois constraints. It was all so confusing, and I couldn't make sense of it. All I knew was I wanted to make love with Heather, and she wanted to make love with me, and I wasn't able to close the deal. So I decided that I must have some sort of psychosexual problem. And that I needed help. I just didn't know where to find it.

In the meantime, I threw myself into my work, and my career took off. A few months after my affair with Heather ended, I was offered a copywriting job at a larger, full-service agency by their creative director, Terry MacDonald. I met Terry the previous year when I took a creative concepts course he taught through the Advertising Club of Greater Boston. I liked Terry a lot, and he liked the work I did in his class. So I jumped at the opportunity to work for him. Not only would it mean getting away from the painful memories associated with The DR Group, but it would also give me a chance to move beyond the constraints of direct mail advertising into the more exciting realms of print, radio, and TV, which is what drew me to the ad biz in the first place.

Like Brian Turley before him, Terry became a mentor and a friend, and he helped me become a rising star in the Boston ad scene. Soon, I was winning Hatch awards, which were handed out at an annual gala celebrating creative excellence in all types of advertising produced by agencies throughout New England. It was like the Academy Awards for copywriters and art directors.

In addition to providing thrills and ego-gratification, winning Hatch awards came with some tangible benefits. The agencies that did well got free publicity, which impressed their clients and helped their new business efforts. And the individuals who had big nights were often rewarded with promotions, raises, and recruiting calls from headhunters and other agencies.

In 1983, I had one of those nights. I won eight Hatch awards, most of them for Paine Furniture, a stuffy, old-line Boston retailer for whom we created a hip new image in a series of irreverent, full-page newspaper ads that ran in the *Boston Sunday Globe Magazine*. They were aimed at all the yuppies who, like me, were moving into Boston's Back Bay and South End and buying furniture for their lofts and condos. Winning those awards was beyond thrilling, and like all thrills, it flooded my brain with shots of adrenaline and dopamine. Together with my art director partners and other colleagues, we celebrated our big night by going out for drinks after the show. But when I woke up the next morning, the excitement had faded, along with the hormones, and the thrills had been replaced by a gnawing sense of emptiness, confusion, and doubt. I felt like the little kid who found that special toy he wanted under the tree on Christmas morning but was bored with it by the end of the day. Or like Robert Redford in the final scene of *The Candidate*. Redford plays a political outsider running for U.S. Senate against a popular incumbent. Although he's given no chance of winning, he somehow manages to eke out a late-night, razor-thin victory. In the wee hours of the morning, with his supporters celebrating all around him, Redford pulls his campaign manager aside and says, with a look of confusion and desperation in his eyes, "What do we do now?"

That's exactly what I was asking myself. What do I do now that I've won all these awards? In order to prove my big night wasn't a fluke, I'd have to keep winning awards. Which felt like pressure. At the same time, I experienced the natural letdown that followed the high of winning. I looked at the award certificates and the Paul Revere bowls I brought home the night before and thought, *What am I supposed to do with these? Put them in a trophy case? What does it all mean, anyway?*

Since I couldn't come up with any answers, I stopped thinking about it and went back to work.

But those unsettling thoughts didn't go away, and they were still haunting me four years and two ad agencies later when I was in New

York shooting that TV commercial for the computer company that helps you "Take it to the limit."

By then, however, I was meeting with Jonathan, my therapist, and was having insights into why I was so confused about what I wanted to do with my life. I was also meditating every day and learning more about Buddhism, which helped me have even deeper insights into why my life felt so unsatisfying. I could see I was lost in the dream-like illusion that temporary pleasures such as winning awards, making money, and having great sex could bring permanent happiness.

Thanks to my experiences in meditation and psychotherapy, I realized that constantly seeking more of these temporary pleasures could never be a path to mental health and inner peace. And while I wasn't willing to shave my head and become a Buddhist monk, I decided that helping others discover some of the deepest truths within themselves would be a better way to spend the rest of my time on this planet.

So finally, one day in late 1987, although not completely confident about my decision, I walked into my boss's office at that big Boston ad agency and told him I was quitting my job so I could go back to school and become a psychotherapist.

PART TWO

Tossing & Turning

CHAPTER TEN

On the Road to Recovery

Before I could find the courage to leave the big Boston ad agency, I had to get my personal life in order. When my affair with Heather came to its ignominious end, I was wallowing in self-pity and hopelessness. I was too embarrassed to discuss it with anyone, and I completely dropped out of the dating scene, for I was certain my problems in the bedroom would continue. I couldn't even imagine being in a healthy, loving relationship with a woman. Before things got worse, I had to find someone who could help me figure out why I was in such a sorry state – and how I could get myself out of it.

But I didn't know where to turn. At that point, I'd never been in therapy, and as far as I knew, no one in my family had either. How to find a therapist wasn't something I wanted to discuss with them anyway. Instead, I asked a good friend who happened to be a clinical social worker for a referral. He gave me the number of a therapist named Roxanne, who ran a small counseling center on the first floor of a two-family house near Harvard Square. It was called New Beginnings.

When I arrived for my first appointment, Roxanne greeted me warmly and asked me to sit down in her cozy office, which was decorated with beanbag chairs, Marimekko prints and posters with inspirational sayings on them. The atmosphere was casual and New Agey, which was fine with me. Roxanne was wearing corduroy jeans and a sweater, and she looked to be a few years older than me. She had wavy brown hair and a slim, athletic body. She also seemed comfortable in her own skin and exuded an air of confidence and well-being. After I told her my sad story, I asked if she could help me.

"Well," she said, "I'm not taking individual clients right now. But there's an opening in my Wednesday night group. And since you're concerned about relationships, group therapy might be a better choice for you. What do you think?"

"Gee, I don't know," I said. "That wasn't what I had in mind. Can I think about it?"

"Sure, just let me know by the end of the week, OK?"

After I promised to get back to her, she said I might also want to consult with a sex therapist, and she gave me the number of a place called Sexual Health Centers of New England. I said I'd have to think about that, too. Then we both stood up to say goodbye, and she gave me a big hug, which made me a bit uncomfortable but also, I had to admit, felt good.

The idea of seeing a sex therapist sounded outlandish and impractical, especially since I didn't have a partner. But performance anxiety in the sexual arena was my most pressing concern, so I decided to look into it. As it turned out, an office of Sexual Health Centers of New England was just a short walk from the ad agency where I was working at the time. So I called and made an appointment.

A week later, I walked over there during my lunch hour and met a psychologist I'll refer to as Dr. Feelgood. The good doctor shook my hand and led me to his office, which had a distinctly clinical feel. Wearing a navy-blue blazer over a white turtleneck, Feelgood was overweight and probably in his mid-forties. He was also sporting a neatly trimmed goatee. As he sat down behind his desk, I noticed two posters with detailed illustrations of the male and female genitalia on the wall behind him, but quickly looked away. Then he picked up a clipboard and asked if I'd be willing to answer some questions about my current situation as well as my sexual history. I swallowed hard and agreed.

After I told him about my sexual performance problems and assured him I wasn't suicidal, Feelgood filled me in on his background, emphasizing that he'd studied with William Masters and Virginia Johnson, the renowned sex researchers who helped jumpstart the sexual revolution of the '60s and '70s. This impressed me. Then he reached into the bottom drawer of his desk, pulled out a model of an erect penis, and demonstrated, to my amazement and embarrassment, something called the squeeze technique, which he said might be part of my treatment plan. It's a method Masters and Johnson developed to delay ejaculation, and it requires the man to take a brief time-out when he feels like he's about to climax so he can squeeze the underside of his erect member until the feeling subsides. Feelgood also said that since I didn't have a partner, he could match me with one of the surrogate partners who worked at the clinic. Then he asked if I'd like to schedule an appointment to meet with a surrogate. I hesitated, mostly because he sounded more like a used car salesman than a mental health professional. Sensing my ambivalence, he said if I didn't get help, I'd probably be plagued by sexual problems for the rest of my life. Since this was my worst fear, I scheduled the appointment and told myself I could cancel if I decided not to go through with it.

When I arrived for my appointment the next week, I met Charlene, my surrogate partner, who escorted me to her office, which was a few doors down the hall from Dr. Feelgood's. It had a much warmer, more welcoming atmosphere than his. We sat down in two comfortable armchairs next to a futon sofa that, she told me, could become a full-size bed. I also noticed some colorful abstract paintings on the walls and a tiny desk in the corner. Charlene was around my age, maybe a little older, with a mop of curly blonde hair on top of the trim body of a yoga instructor. She told me she was getting a PhD in psychology and was doing this work because she was interested in the topic, and because the income helped cover the cost of her education. She also asked questions about my history and what I hoped to get out of the experience. She explained that during this first meeting, we'd just talk, but over the next several weeks, we'd gradually become more and more intimate physically until we felt we were ready to have intercourse, for which we'd use a condom. Charlene seemed comfortable with the whole idea and confident she could help solve my problem. I didn't know how it was going to feel and had major doubts about whether it would work, but I figured it was worth a try.

A week later, I was back in Charlene's office, and in addition to more talking, we did some non-sexual touching exercises – putting our palms together, looking into each other's eyes, standing back-to-back and moving together from side to side – while fully clothed. As the weeks went by, the clothing started to come off, things became more sexual, and I became more comfortable with Charlene and more confident in myself. We also tried the squeeze technique, which I'd been practicing at home. Finally, around week six or seven, we decided it was time to have sex. And when we were done, I felt a sense of relief and happiness. It hadn't been anything like the lovemaking I experienced with Anita back in college, but that was understandable. At least I'd recovered my ability to function.

In any event, Charlene said I was cured and advised me to "go out there and have lots of sex with lots of different women." That sounded like a great idea, but somehow, I didn't think my inner altar boy would go along with the plan. Besides, one good woman was all I wanted.

So instead of running out to the nearest disco or combing through the personal ads in the *Boston Phoenix*, I circled back to Roxanne at New Beginnings. I told her I'd contacted Sexual Health Centers and was feeling better about life in general and my sex life in particular. Then I thanked her for the referral and said I'd like to join one of her therapy groups. She said she was happy for me, that there was still room in her Wednesday night group, and that I could come to a meeting the following week.

When I showed up for that meeting, Roxanne introduced me to the four women and three other men in the group. They ranged in age from their early twenties to late forties, and they all had relationship issues of one sort or another. I didn't know what to expect but was impressed with the way Roxanne ran the group. Looking back on it now, I realize that her methods were, at best, unconventional. Instead of allowing group members to interact more-or-less freely with each other and interrupting only to offer helpful commentary or to keep things from getting out of hand, Roxanne was the star of the show. Each 90-minute meeting began with a go-round, which gave everyone a few minutes to check in and say how they were feeling. Then Roxanne would either ask for a volunteer or select someone to do some intensive one-on-one work with her while the rest of us sat back and watched. Each week, one or two group members would have a turn in the spotlight. Instead of group therapy, it was more like individual therapy with an audience. And it was quite a show. Roxanne was charismatic and intuitive, with a knack for zeroing in on each member's issues. She pushed people to express their hidden feelings, which often led to dramatic moments, with the featured contestants pounding on pillows, shouting obscenities, or breaking down in tears.

For the first two meetings, I just watched. But when I arrived for meeting number three, I was thinking it might be my turn to be part of the evening's entertainment. As usual, we were sitting in a circle, either on beanbag chairs or on the carpeted floor. After the check-in, when no one volunteered to take the spotlight, Roxanne looked at me with a twinkle in her eye.

"How 'bout you, Tom?" she asked with a smile. "You said you've been having trouble in your relationships with women. Would you like to find out why?"

Even though I was half expecting it, I didn't feel ready to spill my guts in front of a group of people I barely knew. So I hesitated and made a face like I'd just swallowed sour milk.

"C'mon," Roxanne prodded, as the others chimed in with words of support.

"Well, I'm here," I finally said, surrendering to the pressure, "so I guess I'll give it a try."

"That's the spirit!" she said as the two of us moved to the center of the circle and sat down on the floor while the onlookers voiced their approval.

"OK, then," she said, waiting for the room to quiet down. "You know, problems in romantic relationships are almost always rooted in our early relationships with our parents. So tell me, what was your mother like?"

I couldn't believe she was bringing my mother into this. *Typical shrink*, I said to myself.

"Well, I know she cared about me," I offered tentatively.

"And how do you know that?"

"She wanted me to get good grades, make good choices..."

"And be a good boy, right?"

"I guess so... "

"Which you always were, right?"

"No, not always. Like if I brought home a report card with all A's and a B, she'd point to the B and say, 'What happened here?'"

"And how did that make you feel?"

"Disappointed. Like I wasn't good enough."

"So she was hard to please."

"Yeah, I suppose she was. I felt like she always looked at me with a critical eye. She'd get upset if my hair wasn't combed right or if I my shirt wasn't tucked in. Stuff like that."

This went on for about fifteen minutes as Roxanne continued to build a case against my mother. And as I listened to her, I remembered the feeling of anxiety that pervaded my childhood home. How insecure I often felt. How it seemed like nothing I did was ever quite right. Then Roxanne brought our interaction to a climax by pushing me back toward the floor, climbing on top of me and putting her hands around my throat.

"Don't you see what was going on?" she asked. "Your mother was critical and controlling. She was suffocating you. She probably didn't feel like she was good enough herself, and she was putting that on you. She wouldn't let you breathe," she hissed as she tightened her grip on my throat. "But she's not in charge anymore. So what are you going to do about it?"

Struggling to catch my breath, I finally shouted, loud enough for everyone to hear, "Get the hell off me! Now!" And I pushed her to one side.

As soon as I did that, Roxanne stood up, smiled, and said to me and the rest of the group, "Now that's more like it."

Did I mention she was unconventional?

It was a powerful but disturbing experience. I felt good about how it ended, but uneasy at the same time. Like I'd been manipulated. I mean, Roxanne never met my mother, right? So how could she be so sure about all those accusations? I continued showing up for the group, however, and as the weeks went by, I started feeling better about myself. I was loosening up. Gaining more confidence. Not feeling so alone. At first, I didn't think I had much in common with the others in the group, but as I heard their stories and shared some of mine, I felt a sense of kinship, like we were all in this together, and that even though we were all different, and we all had our issues, we were all basically OK.

For her part, Roxanne was supportive and helpful. She also brought in some unusual new ways for us to understand and resolve our problems. First it was insights from the world of astrology, which held no interest for me. Then it was something called rebirthing, which she encouraged us all to try. Rebirthing started on the West Coast by a man named Leonard Orr, who with his colleague Sondra Ray published *Rebirthing in the New Age* in 1977. Essentially, it's a controlled breathing technique that induces an altered state in which the participant can supposedly heal past traumas, all the way back to the primal trauma of birth. It's often done in group settings, and Roxanne said she was going to lead a group rebirthing session at New Beginnings on an upcoming Saturday afternoon. I was skeptical, but since I wanted to be open to new ideas, I signed up.

When I arrived on the appointed Saturday, the group room at New Beginnings had been transformed into something that resembled my image of an 19th-century opium den, with low lighting, overstuffed pillows and Indian bedspreads strewn across the floor, and sitar music droning softly in the background. There were about a dozen participants, none of whom I'd met before. In addition to Roxanne, two other therapists from the New Beginnings staff were there to assist. After some opening remarks, Roxanne asked us all to find a spot, lie down, and close our eyes. She assured us that she and her assistants would be available if we had any questions or encountered any difficulties. Then she turned the music up and the lights down, and she told us to breathe rapidly in and out with no pauses between the in-breath and the out-breath, and to keep this going as long as we could. The natural result of this circular breathing, I'd learn later, is hyperventilation, which affects consciousness and perception. I was anxious about doing and possibly *over*doing it, but I was also curious about what might happen.

After a while, I relaxed into it and found myself an altered state. I had also moved, almost involuntarily, into a fetal position. It felt strange, and I didn't know what to make of it. Was I returning to the womb? I actually started laughing as that thought occurred to me. I also heard moans, sobs and other sounds coming from the other folks in the room, along with whispered words of encouragement from Roxanne and her assistants. As I continued the circular breathing, I got in touch with repressed feelings of fear and anger, which dissolved as I breathed through them. One of the assistants came by to put a blanket over me, help me talk through what was happening, and assure me that it was all OK. And it was. In fact, it was all quite extraordinary and for the most part enjoyable. As the session came to an end and the room was filled with the joyous sounds of Pachelbel's Canon, I felt happier, lighter, and more relaxed than I'd felt in a long time. I thanked the assistant and asked how much time had gone by, expecting her to say twenty or thirty minutes. When she said two hours, I was shocked.

Roxanne wrapped things up by thanking us and letting us know that New Beginnings was going to offer individual rebirthing sessions with members of her staff to anyone who was interested. I called on Monday and made an appointment.

My personal rebirther turned out to be Arielle, a clinical social worker and one of the therapists who worked for Roxanne. This was good news. Although I'd never met her, I'd seen her around New Beginnings and thought she was not only pretty, but also seemed like a nice person. She was tall and willowy, with wavy blonde hair and blue eyes. She had a big smile and a ready laugh. She was also one of the gentlest people I'd ever met. After getting to know her a couple of years later, my grandmother said, "That girl wouldn't hurt a fly." And she was right. My first rebirthing session with Arielle went well, and when she asked if I'd like to schedule another, I took a chance and said I'd rather go out to dinner with her instead. She paused, seemed surprised, then said she'd have to ask Roxanne about that and would get back to me.

A few days later, she called.

"Well," she said with a nervous laugh, "Roxanne said we could go out if we want to, but you'll have to be assigned to a different rebirther."

"That's no problem," I said. "Let's do it."

All I can say for sure about what happened next is that it happened fast. Our dinner date went well. And after our second date, we spent the night together. Which felt good. We shared a strong mutual attraction, which I now believe was fueled more by overlapping needs than by a deep and abiding love. But at the time, I grabbed it and clung to it like a drowning man who'd been thrown a life preserver. Within the next few weeks, Arielle more or less moved into my apartment in Brookline, and she soon followed me to the house I was in the process of buying in Boston's Dorchester neighborhood.

Roxanne seemed delighted that Arielle and I had become a couple, and she invited me to join the New Beginnings family by becoming part of her volunteer staff. I agreed and started going to Monday night staff meetings, which were attended by all her paid employees and volunteers, including her husband, an accountant who kept the books. I figured I was brought in because she thought I could upgrade

New Beginning's marketing efforts. In fact, I soon agreed to write a New Beginnings brochure, which my friends at the ad agency agreed to design and print, free of charge. I was happy to do this because Roxanne had us all believing that the work we were doing at New Beginnings was making the world a better place. And I was proud to be part of the growing New Beginnings family.

This idea of family was something else Roxanne liked to promote. She'd sometimes invite staffers to have dinner with her and her husband at their home in Watertown, or to join them in running a 10K race, after which she'd drop a comment like, "You know, this family is a lot healthier than the families we all grew up in." To which everyone would nod in agreement.

Personally, I wasn't so sure about that, but I'd nod anyway, mostly because I was enjoying myself, didn't want to make any waves, and was willing to suspend disbelief.

The first sign of trouble came on a Sunday evening when Arielle and I were invited to dinner at Roxanne's house. We had visited my parents that day, and because we weren't sure how to get to Watertown from Chelmsford, we got lost and arrived fifteen minutes late. We explained what happened and apologized to Roxanne and her husband, which they graciously accepted. But after dinner, as the four of us were taking a walk around their neighborhood, Roxanne pulled the two of us aside and said, "I just want you guys to know that I don't allow the people in my life to be late. So I'm willing to let it go tonight, but if it ever happens again, this'll be the last time you get invited over here."

Arielle and I apologized again but were taken aback. On the way home, we discussed the incident and agreed that it felt threatening, especially since Roxanne was Arielle's employer.

"Maybe she was just trying to model healthy, assertive behavior," Arielle suggested.

"I don't know," I said. "It didn't feel healthy to me."

Later that summer, Arielle and I joined Roxanne and her staffers, both paid and volunteer, together with many of their significant others, for the first-ever New Beginnings staff retreat. This weeklong event took place in a big house Roxanne had rented on Cape Cod. The agenda, according to Roxanne, was for all of us to be on our own during the day, have dinner together every night, then meet after dinner to discuss future directions for New Beginnings and engage in exercises designed to promote personal growth. Roxanne was excited about it and had us all looking forward to it. But it turned out to be a real shitshow.

As the retreat went on, it became increasingly clear that at New Beginnings, Roxanne was the queen and the rest of us were her court. At the big dinner table, she'd scold people for being late or for having side conversations while she was talking. At the nightly meetings, she'd tell us what we needed to do in order to become better people. One night, it was my turn. I hadn't been sleeping well, and Roxanne told me I worried too much about not getting enough sleep. So to help me get over it, she gave me an assignment: Stay up all night, that very night, and don't even try to sleep. I didn't want to do it, but reluctantly agreed. And Arielle, bless her heart, said she'd stay up with me. It turned out to be a long, uneventful night that didn't prove anything except that we were becoming more and more willing to do whatever Roxanne asked of us.

Before we drove back to the Boston area, a few of us shared our concerns about Roxanne's behavior and our fears that New Beginnings was becoming a cult. But no one was willing to challenge her directly and nothing changed.

The turning point for me came the following winter. By this time, Arielle and I were engaged to be married. And we volunteered, along with other staffers, to assist at a weekend workshop for couples Roxanne was leading at a retreat center in central Massachusetts. Arielle and I drove out there early Saturday morning and did whatever we could to help during the first day of the retreat. That night, everyone was staying at the retreat center. But since there weren't enough rooms to go around, Arielle and I spent the night at a local motel.

We didn't sleep much that night, thanks to a noisy party in the next room. When we got up in the morning, we were surprised to see almost a foot of snow on the ground. And it was still snowing hard. We had to get back to the retreat, so we dug out my car, a 1979 AMC Spirit that was notoriously bad in the snow. The main road was in decent shape, but the long side road that wound its way for a mile or so up a big hill to the retreat center was covered with snow and ice. We tried valiantly to negotiate that hill, but kept fishtailing, spinning our wheels, and skidding off the road. It was scary. Lord knows we were willing, but the AMC Spirit was weak. So we turned around, stopped at the motel to phone in a message for Roxanne at the retreat center, then headed back to Boston, where the storm had been mostly rain.

When Arielle went to work on Monday, Roxanne was furious. She said we didn't try hard enough to make it up that hill, and she considered our decision to go home a sign of disloyalty. There was probably a germ of truth in that. Personally, I was getting tired of taking orders from Roxanne, and I think Arielle was, too. I had already dropped out of her therapy group, mostly because of my relationship with Arielle, who was not only Roxanne's employee but also the individual therapist for several members of the group. That put me in an awkward position, especially if I wanted to talk about Arielle in the group. Roxanne didn't seem to care about that, but I certainly did. When I heard about how angry she was at us for putting our safety ahead of our commitment to her, I had enough. I resigned from the staff and cut all my official ties to New Beginnings.

That was fine for me. But Arielle still worked there. And literally overnight, her status changed from one of Roxanne's personal favorites to *persona non grata*. In their therapy sessions – yes, Roxanne was Arielle's therapist in addition to being her employer and friend, which even I knew was a major violation of professional boundaries – Roxanne advised her to break up with me. Arielle told me about this and agonized over what to do. She was clear about wanting to stay together with me. But she didn't know if she could keep working at New Beginnings under such difficult conditions. She finally resigned, which was a huge decision, for it meant losing not just her job, but her therapist and many of her friends as well. The whole experience was traumatic, and she wasn't sure what to do next. Fortunately, she found a new therapist, and soon after that landed a job working at a community mental health center in Worcester, a blue-collar city about an hour west of Boston. I realized I'd better look for another therapist, too, and that's when I found Jonathan, who was helpful in many ways and continued to work with me, off and on, for about six years.

But Arielle continued to struggle. At home, she seemed preoccupied and distracted. She wasn't smiling much anymore. Although she didn't want to go back to New Beginnings, she missed being a part of it. I had to admit that I did, too, and I realized that part of what attracted me to Arielle in the first place was her connection to that warm, loving, supportive, but misguided community of seekers and helpers. I still cared about her, but I wasn't sure my feelings were strong enough to endure the inevitable tests a marriage presents. I was afraid to tell her, however, especially since she was in such a vulnerable state. The first time I mentioned my concerns was in an introductory meeting with one of her prospective new therapists. It was one of two meetings Arielle had scheduled with two therapists who were recommended by a colleague. And she wanted me to come along for moral support. This first therapist was an older woman who seemed competent and professional. As Arielle described what happened to her at New Beginnings, she began to cry softly. The therapist listened empathically, asked a few questions, then turned to me and asked, "What do you think about all this?"

"Well, I was affected by it, too," I said. "In fact, I'm very confused, and I've been wondering if maybe we should postpone our plans to get married until we figure this out."

As soon as she heard this, Arielle said, "Oh, no!" and her soft cries turned into loud sobs.

The therapist looked at me sternly and said, "This is not the time or place to bring up something like that!" And she tried to comfort Arielle.

Looking back on it now, I can understand why the therapist did what she did. After all, this wasn't a couples session. She was trying to protect Arielle as well as keep the focus of the session on her prospective new client. But I felt chastened.

As it turned out, Arielle chose the second therapist, a man whom I also met and who seemed like a better choice to both of us. Then I decided to put my doubts aside and stick with the commitment I made to marry and support Arielle.

The wedding was scheduled for May 8, 1982. It was going to be a modest affair, at least by my family's standards. This was mostly because Arielle wasn't on good terms with her parents, and she wanted us to pay for the wedding ourselves. In fact, a few years before we met, she legally changed her name from Debra to Arielle to signal the distance she was trying to create from her family of origin. This "rebirth" was inspired by Roxanne, who had changed her name from Maureen to Roxanne for similar reasons. I had met Arielle's parents just once when we spent a weekend with them at their home in a sub-urb of Philadelphia.

The next time I saw them was two months before the wedding, when they came to Boston so her mother could attend a bridal show-er my mother planned for Arielle. As the two of us drove to the event, I was alarmed by how nervous she seemed. After we arrived, I was even more alarmed by how much she was drinking and how tipsy she was by the end of the afternoon. When I said something about it on the way home, we got into a nasty argument. But we made up the next day and I chalked the whole thing up to pre-wedding jitters.

Those jitters intensified over the next few weeks. Of course, Arielle's parents were coming to the wedding. But they also wanted us to invite her aunts and uncles and some of their friends. Arielle was against the idea. After a series of phone calls with her mother and some pleading from me, she relented and said the aunts and uncles could come. Then her mother called and said she wanted us to attend a party the night before the wedding at the hotel where the out-of-town relatives were staying. This time Arielle put her foot down and said absolutely not. I was listening from the next room and heard only Arielle's side of the conversation, but based on what she told me after she slammed down the receiver, I believe it went something like this:

"No, Mom, I need to rest the night before the wedding."

"But honey, they're coming all the way to Boston to see you."

"I don't care, Mom. Besides, I'll see them the next day at the wed-ding and the reception."

"But so many other people will be there. This will be a chance to spend some time with your family."

"Goddamn it, Mother. This is your dysfunctional family, not mine. And I don't want to spend time with them. I didn't even want them coming to the goddamn wedding!"

"Well, if that's the way you feel about it, then I'm going to call them all up and tell them not to come."

"That's fine with me. And if that's what you're going to do, then I'm telling you right now that I don't want you and Dad to come either."

"What? You don't want your parents to come to your wedding?"

"That's right! I don't want you to come! You're no longer invited!"

"Fine. If that's what you want, then we're staying home."

"Good!"

"Just don't ever ask for anything from us again. I can't believe you're doing this to us. What in the name of God has happened to our little Debbie?"

"Good-bye, Mom."

(CLICK)

Arielle was shaken when she told me what happened. I begged her to reconsider, but she wasn't about to change her mind.

On the day of the wedding, we got up early and went for a run around our Dorchester neighborhood. It was a gorgeous spring day, warmer than normal for early May. The tulips were in bloom, and the cherry tree in front of our house was bursting with pink blossoms. After the run we showered, ate breakfast, and got dressed. Arielle looked beautiful in the simple, white peasant wedding dress she'd chosen, and she had a ring of spring flowers in her hair. As we got into my car and headed toward Memorial Church in Harvard Yard, where the ceremony was about to begin, we were excited and nervous, happy and sad.

We had told my parents about Arielle's argument with her folks, and her decision to disinvite them. Of course, they were concerned, but there wasn't much they could do. We assumed they shared the news with others in my extended family. When we drove up to the church, many of the guests were still outside, taking in the sunshine. As we got out of the car, my father approached us with a pained look on his face, put his hand on my shoulder, and said softly, "Arielle's parents are here. They're sitting by themselves in the back of the church. What would you like us to do?" Arielle and I were stunned. It never occurred to us that they might crash the wedding.

The minister, a friend of ours and a former New Beginnings client who'd been briefed on the situation, was a step behind my father. Before we could respond to my father's question, he said to Arielle, with great earnestness, "If you want me to ask them to leave, I will."

I turned to Arielle. This was her call. And she didn't hesitate to make it. "Oh, no," she said, "if they're here, then let them stay."

My father asked if he could move them to the front of the church where he and my mother would be sitting. Arielle agreed and gave him a flower from her bouquet to use as a makeshift corsage for the mother of the bride.

After the ceremony, we formed a short reception line – the bride and groom along with our four parents – on the steps of the church. When the crowd thinned out, Arielle and I urged her parents to join us for the reception at a nearby hotel, but they declined, saying they were packed and ready to drive back to Philadelphia, and that they were there only because they wanted to see their daughter get married.

It was a day of mixed and complicated emotions: joy, sadness, excitement, embarrassment, anxiety, relief, and above all, at least for me, confusion. Once again, Arielle drank more than she should have at the reception, and I didn't know what to think about that. But under the circumstances, it was understandable. We left the next day for a honeymoon in St. Maarten, which gave us a chance to rest, reconnect, and forget everything we'd been through prior to and during the wedding. When we returned to Boston, Arielle resumed having occasional phone conversations with her parents, but continued to keep them at a distance emotionally as well as physically. I never saw them again.

For the next year or two, we tried our best to be a happy couple. We completed a series of do-it-yourself home improvement projects that we took on together, and which gave us a sense of pride and shared accomplishment. We also made friends with some of our new neighbors and a few of my colleagues from the world of advertising. And we stayed in touch with some of our old friends from New Beginnings, who told us that Roxanne had gotten herself into some serious trouble. She'd been caught having an illicit sexual relationship with one of her male clients, was being sued by the client's wife, and was about to lose her professional license. This was somehow not surprising, and in spite of ourselves, we couldn't help but feel a giddy sense of schadenfreude.

But Arielle continued to be depressed. She wasn't crazy about her new job, and she didn't like the long commute to Worcester. She'd been a smoker since before we met, which I wasn't happy about, and she began smoking more and more. She even started smoking in bed, which I didn't like at all, especially when I started finding burn holes in our sheets and pillowcases. Afraid she was going to start a fire, I begged her to stop, but she refused because she said it helped her relax so she could fall asleep. We argued about it, and I finally decided I'd just make sure her cigarettes were out before closing my eyes.

Things really started to unravel when she said she wanted to have a baby. I wasn't completely opposed to the idea, but I didn't think we were ready. To be more precise, I knew I wasn't ready, and because I was starting to question Arielle's ability to take care of herself, I didn't think she was in a position to start caring for a child. But she persisted, and I gave in. What the hell, I thought, maybe having a baby will give her something positive to focus on and help her feel better about herself. So we stopped using birth control and hoped for the best.

After several months of trying with no positive results, my doubts increased and so had her depression. I wanted to go back to using birth control. She didn't. We argued back and forth, but this wasn't something we could compromise on. So this time I insisted, and she gave in. Things settled down, at least for a while. Then one night I went into the bathroom after we made love and saw the case for her diaphragm in the medicine cabinet. Just to be sure, I looked inside. When I saw the diaphragm sitting there, I felt a surge of anger and panic. I rushed back into the bedroom and showed her what I found.

"Oh," she said in a distracted way, "I guess I forgot."

"You FORGOT?" I shouted.

"I'm sorry..."

But sorry wasn't good enough. Something fundamental had changed in our relationship. Did she really forget? Or was she trying to trick me into becoming a father? I didn't know. But I just couldn't trust her anymore. We weren't sure what to do next, so we decided to see if a couples therapist could help us sort things out. It didn't take long. I was finally able to express my doubts about the relationship, both in our therapy sessions and at home with Arielle, which she was understandably upset about. In one of our couples sessions, after I said I wanted to be free to date other people, Arielle said she'd had enough and was done with me. That night, she packed a few things and went to a friend's house.

What I felt after she left, more than anything, was relief. Although I knew where she was staying, I didn't call. Eventually, she called and said she'd thought about it some more and wanted to come back to try to work things out. I said OK, but my heart wasn't in it. We tried but didn't get anywhere. After a few more weeks, I packed my bags and moved in with my brother Paul, who had recently bought a house a couple of streets over from ours.

Several months later, I hired a lawyer and filed for divorce, which Arielle refused to accept. She called and said she wanted to go back to the couples therapist, but I said it was too late for that. I knew she wasn't doing well and was worried about her. One night, she called me from a hospital she'd been rushed to after passing out at the local Walgreen's. She asked me to come see her, and I said I'd be right there. When I arrived, she admitted she had a problem with alcohol and tranquilizers, which she'd been getting for the past few years from an unscrupulous doctor, a pill merchant who'd write prescriptions for anyone willing to pay the price. She was an addict, she said, and she wanted to recover. Then she asked me to come back and help support her.

If I knew then what I know now about substance abuse and recovery, I like to think I would have agreed. After all, I took a vow for better or worse, in sickness and in health. But at the time, I was thoroughly uninformed about the subject and didn't even want to think about it. I apologized and said I hoped she'd get the help she needed, but I wasn't able to provide it.

After that, I stopped hearing from her. I eventually called to tell her I wanted to put the house up for sale and split the profits with her. In return, I asked her to find another place to live so I could clean up the house and put it on the market, which she agreed to do. Fortunately, the real estate market was hot at the time, so the house sold quickly, and we made a nice profit, half of which went to Arielle.

I didn't hear from her again until it was time to appear in court for our divorce hearing about a year later. Knowing about her opposition to the divorce as well as her problems with depression and addiction, I didn't know what to expect. But I was prepared for the worst. Maybe she'd show up under the influence, tell the judge how I abandoned her, and say she didn't want to go through with the divorce. Or maybe she'd still be furious and would excoriate me in front of the court, blame the failure of the marriage entirely on me, and reluctantly accept its demise. Or maybe she wouldn't show up at all. What then?

So I was surprised when she walked in that morning looking better than she did on the day we met. She was wearing a flattering new outfit, sporting a chic new hairstyle, and there was a clarity in her eyes I'd never seen before. She smiled when she saw me, then walked over to me and said, "I just want you to know I think we're doing the right thing, and I'd like to go out for a cup of coffee afterwards if you're up for it." Of course, I agreed.

We sat together in the courtroom, where everything went smoothly, and when it was over, we went out for that cup of coffee. Arielle thanked me for the money I sent, which her friends had told her I'd probably try to keep for myself. She told me she'd started going to AA meetings, had been clean and sober for close to a year, and was committed to her ongoing recovery. She also said she had a boyfriend who was in recovery, too, and that the two of them were living together and doing well.

I couldn't have been more pleased. Or stunned. We finished our coffee and promised to keep in touch. And we did get together a few more times for lunch, until her boyfriend said he didn't like the idea. So we stopped. We haven't communicated with each other since then, but I've heard that the two of them got married and that she continues to do well.

When I said goodbye to Arielle, I was still working at a big Boston ad agency, but I hadn't gone on that TV shoot in New York City yet, or started meditating, or announced I was quitting my job so I could go back to school and become a therapist.

Before getting back to that story, however, I'd like to add a footnote about Roxanne. About two decades after I last saw her, I learned that when she lost her social work license, she closed New Beginnings, moved to another state, and changed her name once again. She then teamed up with her astrological advisor and several of his followers. Working together, they formed a cult-like group called the Open Mind Collaborative and began creating amulets made of semiprecious metals and gemstones that were supposedly infused with energy from advanced beings who lived in a parallel universe. They claimed these amulets possessed special healing powers and sold them to their gullible followers for exorbitant sums. Eventually, they were sued by a group of those followers and were charged with fraud by their adopted state's attorney general. The case was settled when Roxanne and her co-defendants agreed to dissolve the Open Mind Collaborative and pay penalties and restitution to the people they'd defrauded.

When I heard about this, all I could do was shake my head in disbelief. How could intelligent, educated adults fall for such nonsense? Then I remembered what happened to Arielle and me at New Beginnings. I knew from experience that when you're lost and troubled, you're vulnerable to the appeals of charlatans, con artists, sociopaths, and cult leaders. Especially if they're charming and charismatic. Which they usually are.

CHAPTER ELEVEN

One Step Forward, Ten Steps Back

It's the fall of 1998. As I walk toward the classroom with notebook in hand, I count back the years: thirteen since my divorce and ten since I quit my job in advertising so I could go back to school and change careers. Finally, I've taken the first significant step toward that goal. I've enrolled in a developmental psychology course at Lesley University, and I'm about to start my first class. When I enter the classroom and take a seat, I look around and realize I've never felt so out of place in my entire life. I'm almost 45 years old, and my classmates are all in their early to mid-twenties. Just about all of them are female. And most are full-time students in the Master's in Counseling Psychology program, while I'm taking just this one course to see what it feels like to be a student again, seeking the knowledge and skills I'll need to become a therapist.

It feels incredibly strange. And while I sit there waiting for the professor to arrive, two questions race through my mind: "What the hell am I doing here?" And "Am I crazy?"

These questions become so loud and insistent, and their answers seem so obvious, that I feel an overwhelming urge to get up, walk out of the classroom, and never look back. But before I act on that impulse, I pause and take a breath.

Why has it taken me so long to get to this point, and why am I still so unsure of myself? Well, when I quit my job at the ad agency, my plans weren't exactly clear. To become a therapist, I knew I'd have to go back to school. But I didn't know which school, or even what kind of degree to pursue. Should I settle for a master's, or should I go for a doctorate, which would take longer and cost more money? And if I go the master's route, should I get a Master's in Social Work, a Master's in Counseling Psychology, or any of several other master's degrees that could lead to a career as a psychotherapist? It was very confusing, and I needed to figure out which path made the most sense for me.

While I explored the options, I started working as a freelance copywriter to keep some money coming in. And this part of my plan turned out to be easier than expected. Even before I left my job, I got an offer from a small ad agency in the suburbs to work there as a freelancer two days a week. Then the folks at the agency I'd just left asked if I'd be willing to work for them a few hours a week on a freelance basis.

Without even trying, I found myself in an enviable position. I could freelance three days a week and spend the rest of my time figuring out where to go to school and doing volunteer work in a mental health setting to get a sense what that might be like. I could also spend more time exercising, reading and meditating. In fact, now that I had more free time and flexibility in my schedule, I could even go on a meditation retreat.

Until then, I was content to meditate on my own and rely on the instructions and inspiration I found in books. In fact, I avoided seeking a meditation teacher or group. After my experience with Roxanne and New Beginnings, I didn't want to get involved with anything that even remotely resembled a cult. But the more I practiced and read about insight meditation and the Buddhist teachings behind it, the more I realized that working with an experienced teacher and becoming part of a community of practitioners could be helpful. I also learned about a well-known and highly respected meditation center not far from my home in Boston: the Insight Meditation Society in Barre, Massachusetts.

So I sent away for a catalog and signed up for a weekend retreat.

A weekend retreat, by the way, is small potatoes at IMS. Most of their retreats last at least a week. And every fall, they offer a three-month retreat, which usually has a long waiting list. But given my resistance and skepticism, a weekend was more than enough for me.

The retreat I signed up for was led by Larry Rosenberg, who'd eventually become my primary meditation teacher. At the time, I had no idea who he was, and I didn't care. I was fairly sure that IMS wasn't a cult and that the people who taught there could be trusted. All I was looking for was a chance to sit in silence with a bunch of other meditators for an extended period of time under the guidance of an experienced teacher.

So on a Friday afternoon in March of 1988, I drove out to Barre, a quiet, rural community in central Massachusetts. When I arrived, I registered, found my room, and looked around. The place had apparently seen better days but was impressive nonetheless in both size and scope. The main building was a stately, red-brick mansion built in 1912 by a wealthy scion of the town for his family. Later, the Catholic Church took it over, used it as a seminary, and added a chapel for worship services and dormitories for aspiring priests and monks. Then, in the mid-'70s, the church put the property up for sale and three young spiritual seekers, all of whom had spent years practicing Buddhist meditation in Asia, raised the money to buy it. Their names were Joseph Goldstein, Jack Kornfield and Sharon Salzberg. On a shoestring budget, they converted the chapel to a meditation hall and turned the property into a retreat center dedicated to the teaching of meditation in the Theravadin tradition. This style of meditation is known by various names, including vipassana, insight meditation, and mindfulness meditation.

After a light supper, about a hundred other retreatants and I filed into the meditation hall for the opening talk from Larry. At this point, we also entered into "noble silence," which we were expected to maintain for the rest of the weekend, except when we were asking questions of the teacher or interacting with a staff member.

I liked Larry right away. He seemed genuine and had a dry sense of humor. Although he was sitting on a raised platform at the front of the hall with an altar and a large Buddha statue behind him, it was clear he didn't take himself too seriously. I don't remember much of what he said that night, but it was probably something about what to expect while we were there, and how this retreat, even though it was for just a weekend, was a rare opportunity for us to practice more intensively than we can at home, to see more clearly how our minds create suffering, and to discover how we can free ourselves of that suffering. Then he sent us off to bed.

The next morning, we were back in the hall at 5:45 for the first sitting of the day. But instead of sitting, Larry asked us to follow him out the door into the brisk, early morning air. Once we were outside, he told us we were going for a walk, and that instead of thinking about where we were going or where else we'd rather be, we should simply be aware of our feet touching the ground and our bodies moving through space with every step we took. He led us in a procession down one side of the long, semi-circular driveway in front of IMS to the main road, took a left there and kept walking along the side of that road, then led us up the other side of the driveway. We continued walking in silence on this route at a brisk pace for about 15 minutes before we filed back into the meditation hall and sat down on our cushions, benches, or chairs. Larry then asked us to focus our attention on the sensations of breathing at either the tip of our nose or the center of our belly. There was no need to control the breath, Larry said. Just let it come and go on its own. And whenever we noticed that our attention had drifted away, we were to note what took it away, and then gently, without judging ourselves, bring it back to the sensations of breathing. We continued practicing this way in silence, with occasional words of encouragement from Larry, until 6:30. Then he rang the bell, said it was time for breakfast, and encouraged us to keep practicing mindful awareness throughout the meal. Instead of focusing on the breath, however, he suggested we do our best to notice all the smells, tastes, sights and sounds we'd encounter in the dining hall. He urged us to slow down, to really taste our food, and notice all the sensations in our mouths and throats as we chewed and swallowed it. He also suggested bringing awareness to the reactions in our minds as well: Liking this, not liking that. Wanting more of this, none of that. Enjoying the experience of the moment, wishing we could be somewhere else. It didn't matter what was happening or whether it was good or bad, pleasant or unpleasant. Or job was simply being aware of each moment as it arose and passed away – and to keep doing this, as best we could, for the rest of the weekend.

Keeping Larry's instructions in mind, I was able to feel the warmth of the mug of tea I held in my hands, hear the clattering of silverware and plates all around me, taste the plain oatmeal and notice myself wishing I'd added raisins and honey to it. But mostly I just ate because I was hungry and didn't want to make things more complicated than they had to be.

After breakfast, there was a work period, a time when most of us did our "yogi jobs," which were assigned to us when we registered for the retreat. These were simple, manual tasks such as washing dishes, putting food away, cleaning a bathroom, sweeping a floor, chopping vegetables, or vacuuming a carpet. Our jobs were also opportunities to deepen our practice by continuing to pay attention to whatever we were doing moment by moment. For the remainder of the morning, there were alternating periods of sitting and walking meditation, usually accompanied by more instructions and encouragement from Larry, until we broke for lunch, the main meal of the day. Then more sitting and walking until "tea," a light evening meal. Then a Dharma talk in the meditation hall from Larry, during which he discussed some aspect of the Buddhist teachings related to our meditation practice. This was followed by a brief question and answer period. Then more sitting and walking until bedtime at 9:30 p.m.

Most retreats at IMS follow this same structure, whether they're for a weekend, ten days, or three months. The experience can be monotonous. But at the same time, it's amazing to see how much your inner world changes from day to day, hour to hour, or even moment to moment.

During that first weekend retreat, however, my experience was unremarkable. I didn't have any new insights, any major highs or lows, any mysterious visions, or any hints of enlightenment. It was a lot like my daily sittings at home, just a lot longer. So when the retreat ended and I climbed into my car on Sunday afternoon, I was disappointed and glad it was over. I was happy to be heading home. And I didn't think I'd be signing up for another retreat anytime soon.

But then I started the engine, and something surprising happened.

The radio came on. It was tuned to the same rock 'n roll station I'd been listening to during my drive to Barre on Friday afternoon.

But I was so shocked by how loud it seemed, I quickly reached for the volume control and turned it down. Way down.

Then I started driving down Pleasant Street, the scenic country road where IMS is located. As I approached the speed limit of 35 miles per hour, I felt nervous. *Whoa*, I said to myself, *this is way too fast!* I actually thought I might lose control of the car. So I slowed down to 30 and then to 25, which felt more manageable. And a bit weird.

When I got home, I had another unsettling experience. I opened the door to my apartment, turned on the lights, and was startled by what I saw on the walls around me: scuff marks, specks of dirt, streaks of grime, and places where the paint was chipped. At first, I thought someone had broken in and ransacked the place. Then I realized that no, all these imperfections must have been there when I left on Friday, and I'd apparently been living with them for the past three years. I just hadn't noticed them.

Vipassana, the style of meditation I'd been practicing, both on my own and during the retreat, is a word in Pali, an ancient Indian language, that means "seeing things clearly" or "seeing things as they are." On one level, this refers to seeing through the apparent solidity of the material world into the underlying, dynamic, ever-changing, interconnected nature of the universe. That's pretty heavy stuff, and while I understand it intellectually, I can't claim I've seen it for myself. But on another, more mundane level, "seeing things clearly" means seeing what's literally right in front of us in the here and now. And on that Sunday afternoon in my apartment, I was seeing the walls around me more clearly than ever before. Instead of being distracted by ruminations about the past or fears about the future, I was right there, in the moment, fully present, seeing my walls as they were, realizing that they needed to be painted. And that was a revelation.

I also saw that this revelation was a result of the intensive meditation I practiced during the weekend retreat. Although it didn't seem like anything was happening, something obviously was. And it felt like something important.

Which is why I decided I to sign up for another retreat. And maybe consider doing a longer one.

In the meantime, I started going to the Cambridge Insight Meditation Center, which Larry Rosenberg had recently opened. Before founding CIMC, Larry went through a major career transition of his own. After earning a PhD in social psychology from the University of Chicago, he became a professor at Harvard Medical School and at Brandeis University, much to the delight of his Russian-Jewish immigrant parents. But Larry soon grew disillusioned with academia, especially after hearing a series of talks by the spiritual teacher Jiddhu Krishnamurti. He became a follower of the iconoclastic Krishnamurti, but realized he needed a path with more structure and tradition behind it and was drawn to Buddhism. He then practiced with the Korean Zen Master Seung Sahn and the Japanese Master Katagiri Roshi. Later, he worked with the Indian vipassana teacher Anagarika Munindra. When he opened CIMC in 1985, he saw it as sister center to the Insight Meditation Society in Barre. But instead of a residential retreat center focused on intensive practice in a bucolic setting, Larry envisioned CIMC as an urban center where a community of students could learn together, practice together, and discover ways of integrating meditation with their everyday lives.

This appealed to me, mostly because it seemed practical and not at all cultish, so I began taking classes at CIMC and participating in their daylong and weekend retreats. Unlike IMS, CIMC doesn't provide overnight accommodations, so on weekend retreatants you show up on Saturday morning, practice in silence with a bunch of other yo-

122

gis – and under the guidance of a teacher – until early evening, then you go home and resume talking with your family and living your life. Then, bright and early on Sunday morning, you return to CIMC for another day of silent practice.

This is a less intense but still powerful way to practice meditation, to slow things down and see how the mind works, how it clings to pleasant experiences and pushes away painful ones based on the deluded belief it can find a permanent place to rest where there is only pleasure and no pain.

At CIMC, I could also schedule interviews, which are private meetings with a teacher, to ask questions and seek guidance on how to bring the Buddhist teachings to life in today's world. During one of these meetings, I told Larry about my plan to transition from a career in advertising to one as a mindfulness-based psychotherapist. I also told him I'd have to go back to school, and that perhaps the best way for me to bring meditation and psychotherapy together would be going to Naropa University, a Buddhist institution in Boulder, Colorado and getting a Master's in Contemplative Psychology. Expecting him to be enthusiastic about this idea, I was surprised when he paused and looked pensive.

"Well," he finally said. "I think you'll probably make a very good therapist. But I don't think you need to go to a Buddhist university. Just continue practicing meditation, go to the best school you can find for your professional training, and the two will come together on their own."

This turned out to be wise and prescient advice. Over the next two decades, meditation and psychotherapy did come together on their own, not just in my life, but in the wider world. Today, thousands of therapists are using mindfulness meditation as a way to help their clients and themselves. In fact, "mindful" has become such a buzz word that I sometimes cringe when I see it used to market products promising improved health, increased happiness, sounder sleep, and better orgasms. As a former ad man, I recognize that this kind of messaging is the result of skillful copywriters doing their job: overpromising and under-informing.

In any event, another piece of advice from Larry also proved to be pivotal during my career transition. And for some reason, it flashed across my mind when I was on the verge of walking out of that developmental psychology class at Lesley. Before putting on my coat and heading for the door, I remembered something Larry said during another retreat – this one a weeklong – at IMS. He was sitting at the front of the meditation hall, telling the hundred or so yogis gathered there that he knows how challenging retreats can be, that it's common for folks to want to leave, and that a number of people had already confessed to him they were thinking about leaving *this* retreat, even though they had signed up for it, paid for it, and intended to complete it. Their minds were telling them that practicing meditation for so many hours and for seven long days was too difficult, that they weren't up to the task, that they should give up and go home.

What he said to them privately and was now sharing with the rest of us were some simple words of wisdom: "If you find yourself in that painful place of self-doubt, please stick with the mind that brought you here."

So before I walked out of that classroom at Lesley, I remembered Larry's words, took a few deep breaths, and stuck with the mind that brought me there.

And that has made all the difference.

As it turned out, I thoroughly enjoyed that developmental psychology class and found the material fascinating. I was especially impressed – and encouraged – by the work of Erik Erikson, who theorized that human development doesn't end when we reach adulthood but continues in a series of eight stages throughout the course of our lives. At each stage, we face a choice, and the choice we make has a profound effect on our continued development. In my final paper for the class, I decided to focus, not surprisingly, on stage seven, which occurs between the ages of forty and sixty-five. The choice we face at this stage is between generativity and stagnation. If we choose stagnation, we stay stuck in our familiar ruts. But if we choose generativity, we find ways to create or nurture something that will outlive us and/or connect us to the world at large. This can be achieved by launching our children, helping people in need, getting involved with community activities, making and sharing art, or doing anything that contributes to the greater good. As part of my research, I interviewed older adults who had successfully navigated stage seven by finding new careers or new ways to give back to the world. I also came to believe that by transitioning from advertising copywriter to mindfulness-based psychotherapist, I'd be choosing generativity over stagnation.

So did I enroll in the master's program at Lesley? Not exactly. My wife, Christine, a clinical social worker and psychotherapist herself, convinced me I'd have more opportunities with a Master's in Social Work. So I applied to social work school instead.

But I'm getting ahead of myself. Let's go back to my decision to sit a longer retreat.

CHAPTER TWELVE

The Long Retreat

After completing my weekend retreat at the Insight Meditation Society, arranging to have my condo repainted, and taking some classes at the Cambridge Insight Meditation Center, I was ready for the next step: a seven-day retreat at IMS. So in June of 1988, I packed up my car once again and headed for central Massachusetts.

Two of IMS's founders, Joseph Goldstein and Sharon Salzberg, were leading this retreat, and I was looking forward to meeting and learning from them. The prospect of sitting in silence with a hundred strangers for seven days was daunting, however, and I wondered what kind of demons might show up to hijack my efforts to find inner peace. What if I started obsessing about the freelance assignment I had to finish when I got home? Or ruminating about my divorce and wondering why I was having so much trouble finding another partner? Or worrying about all kinds of other things that have nothing to do with meditation?

After checking in and bringing my suitcase to my tiny bedroom, I was assigned a yogi job, which was to serve as the "tea table yogi" for the week. The tea table was in the dining room, and it featured a ten-gallon metal urn filled with steaming hot water. Next to the urn was a line of large glass jars that held a wide selection of loose teas – black, green, and herbal. There were also tea bags, tea strainers, teaspoons, whole milk, skim milk, soy milk, and various sweeteners. Beside the tea table stood a waste basket for trash along with a bucket for compost. Retreatants could stop by anytime during the day – or night, for that matter – and make themselves a refreshing cup of tea, then sit in the dining room and sip it contemplatively. My job was keeping the tea table clean, making sure the urn was filled with hot water, emptying the trash and compost bucket at least once a day, and replacing any teas or other supplies that needed to be replenished.

I was happy to have this job. It was an easy one, and definitely more enjoyable than cleaning a bathroom or mopping a floor. Best of all, it required just a little attention here and there throughout the day, which meant I'd be free during the official after-breakfast work period to go back to my room and relax, take a walk in the woods behind the retreat center, or return to the meditation hall to sit on my cushion.

I never suspected that this job would present me with the biggest challenge – and learning opportunity – of the retreat.

Once the retreat began, I settled into the rhythm of the alternating sitting and walking periods, occasionally interrupted by meals and other breaks. I appreciated the guidance offered by Joseph and Sharon, who exuded wisdom and compassion and seemed totally dedicated to their work as Dharma teachers. Their nightly talks were always helpful and sometimes inspiring. I was especially moved by their allusions to where this meditative path could ultimately lead: To the sublime state of enlightenment, a place of profound understanding and inner peace.

But I was also struggling. At first, the struggles were physical. I was experiencing a lot of back pain, which felt like a big distraction.

The teachers acknowledged that sitting for long periods of time often leads to pain in the body, especially for those who are new to retreat practice. The question then becomes, how do you relate to the pain? Do you shift your posture? Maybe. But that only provides temporary relief. Do you move to a chair if you've been sitting on a cushion or bench? Perhaps. But that feels like giving in. So can you just sit with the pain? Can you get interested in it instead of fighting it? Can you relax into it and notice how it tends to change, becoming more intense, then less intense, disappearing briefly then reappearing somewhere else? Can you see it as simply pain, part of life, and not *your* pain?

For me, even more thorny than the physical pain was the mental suffering that emerged as the retreat lumbered on. Surprisingly, much of this suffering was related to my yogi job. It was a simple job. A plum assignment. But as I performed all the required duties, all by myself, I found myself looking for a pat on the back, a word of thanks, or some other sign of approval. Of course, I didn't expect this from my fellow yogis, who had taken temporary vows of silence. But what about the IMS staff members, who could see me doing my work in the kitchen and dining room? They were free to express their appreciation if they wanted to. At least that's what I thought. Eventually, however, I realized that since I was a retreatant, they weren't supposed to say anything to me or even acknowledge me. When that sunk in, I felt bereft. Because I had become, for lack of a better term, an approval junkie. As a copywriter, I got a recurring charge out of coming up with ideas that others in the agency not only liked, but literally *approved* by adding their initials to the ad layouts that went through the agency chain of command before they were presented to a client. Of course, my ideas weren't always approved. But that made approval, when it did come, even more addictive.

Working as the tea table yogi, I couldn't get the approval I'd grown accustomed to and desperately craved. This was both painful and amusing. At some level I knew I was being silly, and part of me could see this. But I could also see it was one of the reasons I was hooked on the advertising business, which helped me see that kicking the copywriting habit would probably be good for both my mental health and spiritual growth.

Then something even more disturbing happened. I started worrying that maybe I wasn't doing such a good job as the tea table yogi after all. One afternoon, as I sat in the meditation hall following my breath, I realized I hadn't checked the tea table since before lunch. What if it had become an unsightly mess? What would people think of me? These worries and self-critical thoughts filled my mind until the end of the meditation period, when I could go take a look.

"Whew," I said to myself as I entered the dining room and saw the tea table, "everything looks good."

One afternoon later in the week, however, I stopped by to check on things and discovered that the big urn of hot water was empty. I'd let it run dry! Which meant no one was able to get hot water for tea. And I didn't even know how long it had been that way! At this point, I started beating myself up for being so negligent. And after refilling the urn, it took me several shame-filled hours to calm down.

Part of this obsessiveness was due to a phenomenon called "yogi mind." When practicing meditation, especially during a long retreat, it's easy to ruminate about little things you'd normally dismiss, ignore, or not even notice. And it's surprising how painful these little things can become. However, the pain also presents an opportunity to take a good look at your mental and emotional patterns. For me, this retreat was the first time I saw just how much I seemed to need the approval of others, and how this need was fueled by an underlying state of anxiety about not being good enough. I also saw that I'd subconsciously developed a way to get the approval I believed I needed. How? By creating a strong inner critic – an anxious, insistent inner voice whose job was to keep me in line and let me know what I needed to do in order to please all the people in my life. Unfortunately, that same voice could become cruel and abusive when I failed to do what I was supposed to. It could jump in and berate me for how I had messed up. Then it might look back and start recounting my past failures, just to make sure I got the point.

As long as I was able to stay in the present moment by sensing the breath as it flowed in and out, by feeling my feet touching the ground as I walked, by hearing the birds singing outside the meditation hall, I was able to keep this inner demon at bay. And the longer I stayed focused on what was actually happening in the moment, the quieter my mind became and the better I felt. "Ah, this is it," I'd think. "I've finally got it! All I have to do is stay in the present moment and I'll never have to feel anxious or afraid or inadequate – ever again!" My mind would be peaceful and calm, my body would be relaxed and free of pain, and the world around me would appear fresh and alive, at least for a little while. But inevitably, things would change. And the inner critic – whom I eventually named Brutus – would show up to torment me.

Brutus was especially fond of making an appearance whenever my thoughts turned to my relationships with women. For the sad truth was, my love life had always been more painful and problematic than my work life. I'd be sitting in the meditation hall, breathing in and out, feeling relaxed and maybe even a little sleepy, when my mind would drift back, almost imperceptibly, to a past romantic relationship. Like the one I had with Anita, my college girlfriend and first true love. These memories would be pleasant at first. I'd remember how great it was to be with her, how totally in love I was with her, and how totally loved I felt in return. However, I wasn't being mindful of these thoughts. I wasn't just watching them arise and pass away. Instead, I was getting lost in them. This was easy to do because they were all so pleasant. But it was also an invitation for the inner critic to step in. Which would inevitably lead to feelings of guilt, shame, and regret. *"So why did you break up with her?"* Brutus would ask. *"Just because you were starting to get bored and wanted to go out with someone else, someone who wasn't even interested in you? You really blew that one big time! And you broke poor Anita's heart! What the hell is wrong with you?"*

Or I'd think about my marriage to Arielle, a kind and loving person who happened to have a troubled past and a problem with substance abuse. Which made it a more complicated relationship than my idyllic college romance. *"Sure, it was complicated,"* Brutus would pipe in, *"but you were married to her, for Chrissake! And when the going got tough, you walked out on her. She needed help, and you didn't care. You really don't know what love is all about, do you?"*

Then there was the affair with Heather during my time at The DR Group. *"That was the biggest disaster of all,"* shouted Brutus. *"She was married, you idiot! Where was your moral compass? Did you really think it was going to end well? You're lucky you didn't get yourself killed!"*

Brutus loved to pick on me. About big things and little things. I pictured him as this angry, maniacal little man with a long, curly mustache who'd stand on my shoulder with a sledgehammer and punctuate each of his nasty, critical remarks with a vicious blow to the side my head.

I hated that little man. And not just because of what he was saying about me. He was also ruining my retreat! Instead of calmly feeling my breath and staying in the present moment, I was getting carried away by these imaginary dramas that had nothing to do with meditation. Then I'd start hating myself for being a lousy meditator, a bad yogi. I'd look around and see everyone else sitting quietly on their cushions, and I'd assume they were all in states of contentment and bliss. *"Why can't you be more like them?"* Brutus would ask. *"You don't know what you're doing here, do you, pal? Maybe you should just leave!"*

But instead of leaving, I stuck with the mind that brought me there. I stopped listening to the sadistic little man on my shoulder and kept coming back to the breath, or to some other sensation in the body. Gradually, Brutus began to lose interest and fade away. And eventually, I'd realize he was gone. Then I'd feel a rush of euphoria. I'd think, *This meditation stuff really works! And I can actually do it! Everything's gonna be OK!*

And everything *would* be OK. For a while. Until Brutus showed up again, ready to attack. Then the whole process – of suffering, despair, surrender, relief – would begin again.

These ups and downs persisted, with surprising frequency, for the rest of the week. It was exhausting and exhilarating. Before that retreat, I had no idea so much drama could arise all by itself, with little to no input from the outside world. It was all in my head. And I could see it was preventing me from being fully present in my life almost all the time.

This was a sobering but important insight. And as I prepared to leave the retreat, I felt shaken. The ground under my feet didn't seem as solid as I thought it was. I wasn't sure what to do or where to go next. But for some reason, when I got in my car and started driving back to Boston, I took a detour and visited my parents first.

My parents hadn't said much about my interest in Buddhist meditation, but I had a feeling they weren't exactly thrilled with it. After all, they raised me to be a good Catholic. And even though they knew I became disenchanted with the teachings of the church and stopped going to Mass when I was in high school, I assumed they were still hoping I'd see the light and come back to the fold.

As I drove toward their house, I realized I wanted to assure them that the meditative path I was on had real value, that it felt much more alive to me than the gospels and prayers and church rituals I sat through in my youth. I wanted them to know I was learning a lot, not just about myself but about life in general, and they didn't have to worry. In a way, I guess I was seeking their blessing – and, I suppose, their approval.

When I arrived at my parents' house, we exchanged greetings, and I sat down in the family room with them. It was a quiet Sunday afternoon in June. Dad was in his rocking chair, watching the Red Sox on TV. Mom was on the sofa, reading a book, which she soon put down and asked if she could get me something to eat or drink.

"No, that's OK, I just wanted to stop by, say hello, and tell you about the retreat I just finished."

"Well, we'd love to hear about it, right, Pete?" she says to my father, who's cursing at the TV because someone on the Sox has just grounded into an inning-ending double play.

"Right, Pete?" my mother repeats.

"Oh, right!" he finally says, sounding like he's not completely sure what he just agreed with.

So I do my best to describe the retreat to them, and to tell them how deeply I was affected by it. I talk about getting in touch with my inner critic, seeing how much I crave the approval of others, and how this craving is a distraction that prevents me from being more fully present, more fully alive. My mother sits close to me, listening intently, looking perplexed, not knowing how to respond. My father is across the room, only half listening, mostly because he's trying to keep one eye and one ear on the ball game. After a few minutes, I sum it all up with a brief statement that suddenly comes to me and expresses the most important thing I've learned during the past week.

"I can see now," I say with tears in my eyes and regret in my voice, "that I've missed so much of my life. Because I just haven't been present for it."

Seeing the tears, my mother reaches out and asks, "Are you OK?"

"Yes," I reply. "I think I'm more OK than I've been in a very long time."

As I left them that day, I realized they didn't understand what I was trying to say, which was disappointing. And at one point on the drive home, as I thought about the growing distance between my parents and myself, I looked out my window at the wide grassy area between the southbound and northbound lanes of Route 3, the highway that was taking me back to Boston, and I saw hundreds of white and yellow wildflowers waving in the breeze there. I mean I really *saw* those flowers, and I was moved by their beauty. I also felt a kinship with them, knowing that, like me, they were rooted in the earth below while seeking the light above. All I can say for sure is that their unexpected appearance in the middle of this drab, soulless, four-lane highway felt like a gift. A kind of grace. Once again, my eyes filled with tears. Only this time, they spilled over and began rolling down my cheeks.

The week of silent sitting, walking, and paying attention was apparently allowing something in my heart to open.

CHAPTER THIRTEEN

Love & Marriage, Take Two

Meanwhile, back at the office, which was a small desk in the corner of my bedroom, I continued to seek freelance work. Using my first computer, a newly purchased Apple Macintosh, I reached out to my network of advertising colleagues to let them know I was available. And the assignments kept coming in. I was happy to have the business, but I tried to keep my workload manageable so I'd have enough time to pursue my interests in meditating and finding a more meaningful way to make a living.

This little detour would last more than a decade.

Part of the reason I was diverted from my plan to become a psychotherapist was because my life as a freelancer was turning out to be a lot more enjoyable and much less stressful than my life as a full-time ad agency copywriter. As I continued to pick up more work, not just from ad agencies but also directly from some clients, freelancing was turning out to be more lucrative, too. I was working fewer hours, having more fun, and making more money than ever before.

What's not to like about that?

And as I looked into how much I could expect to earn after getting a Master's in Social Work, I learned that starting salaries for MSWs were shockingly low, so the drop in my income would be bigger than anticipated. Plus, that income wouldn't even start until I took two years off to complete – and pay for – a full-time master's program. Did I really want to do that? After all, I still had a mortgage to pay. And I still liked going out to eat once in a while. Yes, I was turned off by the excesses of capitalism as exemplified by the advertising business, but I didn't want to take a vow of poverty. I was also still hoping to find a woman to share my life with, and I was afraid that being a below-average breadwinner might make my search even more challenging than it had already been.

All of a sudden, I wasn't so sure about following through with my plan.

Things got even more complicated when I met the woman who'd become my next – and hopefully, final – wife. This happened at the end of 1991, on the way to the annual 10-day New Year's retreat at the Insight Meditation Society. I signed up for that retreat because it was led by Jack Kornfield. One of the founders of IMS, Jack was also the co-author (with Joseph Goldstein) of *Seeking the Heart of Wisdom,* a book that inspired me when I began my journey on the meditative path. But by 1991, Jack was based in California, where he earned a PhD in clinical psychology and opened his own meditation center. Jack was combining Eastern meditation practices with Western psychology, a combination that spoke to me, and this retreat promised to be a rare opportunity to learn from him, right in my own backyard.

When I sent in my registration, I indicated I could provide a ride to the retreat for another person from the Boston area. A week before the retreat started, I heard from IMS that someone named Christine, who lived in Concord, needed such a ride. Since I had to drive through Concord on the way to Barre, that would be no problem for me. So I called Christine and got directions to her house.

At the appointed hour, I pulled into the driveway of a small white house that looked like it needed painting and other repairs. I walked to the front door and rang the bell.

"Just a minute!" said a female voice. "I'll be right there."

I heard some muffled noises from inside, then the door opened. "You must be Tom," she said, looking just a little frazzled.

"And you must be Christine," I replied.

"Yes, and thank you so much for giving me a ride. But I'm not quite ready, so please come in."

As I entered, I noticed the smell of something burning coming from the kitchen. "Is everything OK?" I asked.

"Yeah, I just left some soup on the stove while I ran out to do a quick errand, and it started to burn. But everything's fine now."

Hmm, I thought. *That's not the most mindful thing to do as you're preparing to go on a meditation retreat, is it?* But I kept that thought to myself.

After Christine gathered her things, we were on our way. During the drive, we chatted and learned more about each other. I told her about my freelance work and my plan to change careers. She told me she was a clinical social worker who worked at a community mental health center, and that she had a small private practice on the side. She also said she'd been practicing various forms of meditation and going to retreats since the mid-seventies.

Christine was attractive, single, and a couple of years older than me. She was also bright and engaging, and the fact that she was a social worker, a psychotherapist, and a serious meditator impressed me. As the ride continued, I started to think that maybe the two of us could become friends, or perhaps even more. But I quickly dropped the idea, partly because I didn't want to think about it during the retreat, and partly because my most recent relationship had ended painfully about a month earlier, and I wasn't ready to jump into another one.

Coincidentally, this prior relationship was with another clinical social worker who worked at a community mental health center. Sara and I met the previous winter through a mutual friend, and after a slow start, we became an item. Or so I thought. Sara was small of stature but large of heart, a modern-day Bohemian, and a free thinker. While I was introspective and reserved, Sara was adventurous and spontaneous, with a ready laugh and a willingness to take chances.

Our differences seemed to complement each other. Over the summer, we went to Montreal for a week and spent weekends together on Cape Cod. She happened to live around the corner from me in the South End, so we often got together during the week as well. Although we hadn't made any promises to each other, I thought we were headed for a long-term relationship. Maybe even marriage.

Then, one evening that fall, Sara calls and asks if she can come over.

I buzz her in and greet her at my door. Instead of giving me the usual hug and kiss, she breezes by me, heads for the living room sofa, and sits down.

"What's up?" I ask as I take a seat beside her.

She pauses, looks at me and says, "We need to talk."

"Okay, what about?"

"About us."

"What about us?" I ask, sensing the bad news that's about to be delivered.

"I know this may come as a surprise," she says, "but I want to take a break from our relationship."

"A break? What's that supposed to mean?"

"I want to go out with other guys."

I'm stunned and hurt and don't know what to say next except, "Why?"

"I've been feeling tied down."

"That's news to me," I blurt out, starting to get upset and feeling that I've been misled. "Why didn't you say something about this sooner? And why are you doing this now?"

She looks away, then back at me. "Well, I wasn't going to mention this, but remember that old boyfriend I told you about, the one whose sister is a movie actress?"

"Yeah…"

"Well, he's been in Europe for the past two years, but he's back in town now, and we got together the other night. And I told him I'd like to see him again."

There's an awkward silence as I let this sink in.

"What about us?" I finally ask, "You're going to end it, just like that?"

After another awkward silence, she answers my question.

"You know, I usually don't give a reason when I break up with a guy, but I think you deserve one." Then she pauses. "You're just too much of a Nervous Nellie for me."

That remark felt like a punch to the gut. I suppose she thought this information might be helpful to me, but it just made me feel worse. I remembered, with regret, the time we were in the Montreal Botanical Garden, and she wanted to venture into an area marked "Keep Out," but I talked her out of it. Then there was the afternoon we were on a quiet beach in Provincetown, and she wanted to make love in the dunes, but I declined because I couldn't stand the thought of being discovered or even observed.

Besides, I already knew I was an anxious guy, a "Nervous Nellie," as she put it, and it wasn't something I was proud of. I also knew it wasn't something I could just snap my fingers and change. After all, I come from a long line of Nervous Nellies. Both my parents were anxious people, and so are all three of my three siblings. We're a family of worriers, not warriors. Anxiety is part of my genetic heritage. I was coming to terms with this in my therapy and meditation sessions, and I was doing my best to accept it. Still, I was upset and disappointed that it had apparently ruined my relationship with this woman I was becoming more and more attached to. I knew I needed some time to grieve and heal.

And I thought that the New Year's retreat at IMS would be a good place to do just that.

Once the retreat began, I continued seeing Christine in the meditation hall, the dining hall, and various other places throughout the retreat center. Of course, we didn't speak to each other. We didn't make any eye contact either, at least not that I can remember. For in addition to remaining silent, retreatants at IMS and other Buddhist meditation centers are advised to avoid eye contact in order to support each other's inner work.

Actually, I didn't even think about Christine much during the retreat as I tried to stay focused on the present moment. But the mind has a mind of its own, and mine kept wanting to ruminate about Sara and other past relationships and what the heck I wanted to do with the rest of my life. And Brutus, my trusty inner critic, continued to make regular appearances, saying things like, *"Nervous Nellie, Nervous Nellie! Why do you have to be so anxious, anyway? Don't you know that women are turned off by anxious guys? Why can't you be a real man?"*

His attacks were painful. But I did my best to put them aside, to redirect my attention to the breath as a way to calm myself and find some semblance of inner peace.

When the retreat ended, Christine and I headed back to my car for the return trip to Concord and Boston. This time, we were with another yogi who needed a ride back to Boston and who, when we told her about halfway there that no, we weren't a couple, said "Really? I'm surprised to hear that. You certainly seem like one!"

When I dropped Christine off in Concord, we gave each other a quick hug and promised to stay in touch. And about a week or so later, after I returned to my usual routine, I decided I wanted to see her again. So I called to ask how she was doing and invite her to my place for dinner the following Saturday, a proposal that wasn't met with enthusiasm.

"Your place…in Boston? But I hate driving into the city," she said. "And what about parking?"

"Don't worry," I assured her. "I'm on a main street. It's easy to find, and you should be able to get a parking spot nearby, especially at six o'clock on a Saturday evening. I've been parking my car on the streets around here for over six years now, and I've never had a problem."

She agreed, somewhat reluctantly, but also said she'd have to leave my place by nine to go ballroom dancing with some friends in Cambridge. That was OK by me.

So she showed up, right on time, and we both enjoyed the tasty vegetarian dinner I prepared for the occasion. We talked about the retreat, learned more about each other, and seemed to feel comfortable in each other's presence. And when the clock struck nine, we both went downstairs to find her car.

She said it was right on the same block as my building. But when we got to the end of the block, we hadn't seen her car.

"Oh, I was distracted because we were talking and I wasn't paying attention," she says. "I must have missed it."

So we retrace our steps, looking more carefully this time, and she still doesn't see it.

"Maybe you parked on the next block," I suggest, as we both feel a growing sense of dread.

She doesn't think so but agrees to check. Then, after walking up and down the next block, and returning to the first block for one last look, we turn and look at each other.

"Do you think it's been towed?" she asks, sounding more than a little upset.

"No... if it was on one of these blocks, it was legally parked, so I'm sure it wasn't towed."

"Then it must have been stolen!"

"Well, that's a possibility..."

"But who would steal that car?" she asks. "It's an old, beat-up, rusted-out Toyota Corolla! One of the turn signal lights is hanging down over the front bumper and the front door on the passenger side doesn't even open!"

"I'm so sorry," I say, sensing her dismay and feeling somewhat responsible because I told her the neighborhood was safe. "I can't believe it," I add. Then I repeat that I've been parking my car on these streets for years without ever having a problem. Which doesn't make her feel any better.

After a few moments of indecision, I suggest we walk to the local police station and report what happened. When we tell the officer on duty our story, he agrees that the car was probably stolen and says the police will try to recover it. But he doesn't sound hopeful. He says that even though it's an old car, it can be worth quite a bit of money in parts. So it'll probably be stripped and end up in a junkyard. Then he asks Christine to fill out some paperwork and sends us on our way.

"What do we do now?" she asks when we're back outside.

"I don't know about you, but I could use a drink," I reply. "Whaddya say?"

"I guess so," she says half-heartedly. "I'm definitely not going dancing tonight."

So we find a local pub and have a drink together. The mood has turned somber, and she's clearly distracted. But I try to stay positive.

"It might've just been some kids out for a joy ride," I say. "The cops'll probably find it in another day or two."

"I don't know. I hope so."

After we finish our drinks, I drive her back to Concord, make sure she gets into her house safely, then drive back to Boston. As I approach the city, I'm thinking that this wasn't the most auspicious way to begin a relationship. On the other hand, maybe it was.

In any event, Christine and I stayed in touch by phone over the next few weeks, and during those calls I began to learn, among other things, how challenging it was for her – or anyone else, for that matter – to make ends meet on a social worker's salary.

"Well, I have to pay the rent, plus all the utilities and the car insurance every month," she told me. "And I'm still paying off my student loans, which doesn't leave me much money to play with. But I manage. I have oatmeal for breakfast, bring peanut butter and jelly sandwiches to work for lunch, and usually make something cheap like soup or pasta for dinner. I get most of my clothes at consignment shops. Oh, and I keep my thermostat at 55 degrees during the day and 45 at night."

"Even now? In January? You must be freezing!"

"Well, during the day I wear lots of layers under a down vest, or I keep my coat on – and I keep moving! At night I sleep in sweats under a pile of blankets with my cat curled up next to me. It's not so bad."

When I asked why she was living in a house in an expensive suburb like Concord, she said it was only because she got an unbelievably good deal from the owner, a woman she met on a canoe trip with the Appalachian Mountain Club. The woman's mother had been living in the house, but because of declining health, was forced to move into a nursing home. Since the house was small and rundown, and because of their AMC connection, the woman was charging Christine about half the market rate.

"But she said she'll have to double the rent at some point, which means I'll have to find a housemate."

She also said she was already looking for her next car. However, she didn't want to buy it until the insurance company declared her Toyota a total loss, which wouldn't happen until thirty days had passed from the day it was stolen. In the meantime, she was driving a rental from Rent-a-Wreck. And her insurance was covering that.

There was another problem. If she waited the full thirty days – plus a few more for the check from the insurance company to arrive – before she bought another car, she'd be on the hook for the cost of the rental car for each day after day number thirty. That could amount to quite a bit. To avoid that expense, she wanted to purchase her next car as close to the thirty-day mark as possible. So on day twenty-nine, after she found a used Nissan Sentra that seemed acceptable and received a loan from her father to pay for it, she signed on the dotted line, turned in her rental, and drove the Nissan to work at the clinic.

Then, as she walked into the office, the receptionist told her she had a call waiting. She took the call, which was from a police sergeant in Lawrence, Massachusetts, who told her that her Toyota Corolla had been recovered and was sitting in a tow lot in his fair city.

This wasn't good news.

The Toyota was found within the 30-day limit, but the insurance company would have to inspect it before they could settle Christine's claim. Fortunately, their claims inspector reported a few days later that the car had been stripped of all valuable parts and was a total loss. Then there was another complication. The car was actually recovered by the tow company just three days after it was stolen. They said they didn't contact anyone because they couldn't read the vehicle identification number. Then, on day twenty-nine, by some apparent miracle, they suddenly *could* read the VIN and called the police, who called Christine. When the insurance company heard about this, they told Christine that since her car had been found on day three, they'd cover just the first three days of the Rent-a-Wreck, and she'd have to pay the rental charges for the other 26 days. To make matters worse, the tow company told her she'd also have to pay a $10-per-day storage fee for the thirty days her car had been on their lot.

Christine was incensed. "This is so unfair!" she said. She was also worried because she simply couldn't afford hundreds of dollars' worth of car rental and storage fees. So she snapped into action. First, she called the insurance company and pleaded her case. Yes, she argued, the car was recovered after three days but she hadn't been told about it until day twenty-nine. So why was she, the unsuspecting owner, being held responsible? The customer service representative said he was sorry, but that's just the way it works. So she asked to speak to that person's supervisor, and then to the customer service manager. All to no avail. Finally, out of sheer frustration, she broke down in tears and pleaded for mercy, "But I'm a poor social worker. I can't afford this!" The manager paused, put her on hold, then came back a few minutes later to say they'd reconsidered and would cover the full cost of the car rental.

After a brief victory dance, she called the tow company and asked them to waive the storage fees they expected her to pay. But they refused to budge. So she contacted her state rep and the local police, who told her that what the tow company was trying to do was illegal. Armed with that information, she called the tow company again and they backed down.

Although I was just a spectator and cheerleader during this debacle, it taught me two important lessons. First, that Christine was a force to be reckoned with. And second, that I had no idea how difficult it was for someone to make ends meet in the Greater Boston area on a clinical social worker's salary.

Actually, this was when I started waking up to the many invisible ways I benefited from being a white, able-bodied, cis-gendered, heterosexual male. Looking back, I can understand why these privileges were hard for me to see. Subjectively speaking, my life always felt like a struggle. It didn't feel like anything was ever just handed to me. I didn't have a trust fund waiting in the wings. I had to work hard to get good grades, to get into a good college, to get a job, to get ahead. And still, even after I achieved some measure of material success, I struggled to be happy with my chosen career, to find love and companionship, to feel like I fit in, to feel like I was OK, like I had enough, like I *was* enough.

What I failed to see is that I had a much better chance of getting into a top college, especially back in 1971, because I was a white male. That I was able to graduate debt-free because my father, another white male, was high enough on the corporate ladder to be able to send all four of his kids to fancy private colleges without the need for student loans. That I had an inside track to landing a job in advertising, a field dominated by white males. That Brian Turley, the first creative director who hired me, was a fellow Harvard alum who told me he loved the Harvard Band when he was a student. That I was probably paid more than my female counterparts. And that one of the reasons social workers' salaries are so low is because the vast majority of them are women.

What I also failed to see is that my struggle to find happiness was just part of being human. In Buddhism, the first Noble Truth is usually translated as, "Life is suffering." Because of this, Buddhism is often thought to have a pessimistic view of our human existence. But I prefer a different, and in my opinion, more accurate translation: "Life as most people experience it is unsatisfying." And why is it unsatisfying? Because we often don't get what we want, which leads to disappointment. And even when do get what we want, it doesn't last, which leads to a different type of disappointment. If we're lucky, life's lack of satisfactoriness is limited to the effects of impermanence, which inevitably leads to disappointment and ultimately to aging, illness, and death. If we're not so lucky, we may also have to endure such calamities as war, genocide, famine, starvation, homelessness, poverty, disability, racism, oppression, trauma, addiction, crime, violence, rape, torture, and imprisonment.

Seen from that perspective, I was one of the lucky ones. And so was Christine. Even though being female and poor were two additional challenges she had to face.

In any event, Christine managed to get the insurance company and the tow company to waive their unfair fees. And although we'd spoken on the phone quite a few times during her long ordeal, we hadn't actually seen each other since the night her car was stolen. So we decided it was time for our second date. And what did we decide to do? Drive up to Lawrence in her new but much-used Nissan, retrieve any of her belongings that still remained in the stripped-down Toyota, and file a report with the Lawrence police.

I don't remember much about that day, except that we found ourselves in a seedy section of a run-down city and discovered nothing of value in the Toyota. Even her cassette tapes of Dharma talks by Jack Kornfield, Joseph Goldstein and other meditation teachers had been stolen. "Well, I hope the thieves listen to them," she said, imagining a way for something positive to result from her misfortune. Somehow, we both found a way to enjoy the day and each other's company. Soon, we found ourselves spending all our weekends together, sharing all the things we had in common and learning about the things we didn't.

About a year later, we decided to move in together. But we needed to find a place. My condo was too small, and she didn't want to live in the city. I didn't want to move to Concord because it was too far from the city, where most of my work was, and because we'd have to share her small house with the roommate she found when the landlord doubled the rent. So we compromised, as all couples must, and bought a house in Arlington, which was about halfway between Boston and Concord – demographically as well as geographically.

We continued to meditate together at home and on retreats at IMS and at CIMC, where we made friends with other practitioners and became part of the community there. And in September of 1994, accompanied by our immediate families and a few guests, we were married during a small, Buddhist-inspired ceremony at CIMC that was officiated by Narayan Liebenson, one of our meditation teachers.

CHAPTER FOURTEEN

Volunteering

After leaving my ad agency job, I started looking for volunteer opportunities that could help prepare me for my second career.

The first I found was with Samaritans, an organization that runs suicide prevention hotlines all over the world. I was drawn to Samaritans because I'd been seeing their ads in various places around Eastern Massachusetts since I was a kid. I remember spotting one of their signs on the Sagamore Bridge, a mighty span connecting Cape Cod with the mainland, each time my family drove across it so we could spend my father's two-week summer vacation in a rented cottage near the beach. It was a stark, simple billboard that said, "Desperate? Need help? Call Samaritans at TOLL-FREE NUMBER." At first, I didn't know what to make of it. But as I got older, I realized that the sign's message was meant for every desperate soul who was contemplating a fatal leap from the bridge to the choppy waters below.

Although talking to people on the verge of taking their own lives sounded daunting, I knew that if I was going to become a therapist, I'd have to learn how to handle situations like that. So I called Samaritans and registered for their volunteer training course. During that course, I learned that our main job as volunteers was listening to the people who called and offering empathy and emotional support. By responding in a non-judgmental way and asking open-ended questions, we hoped to help these callers find a way to move forward in their lives. If, however, we believed that a caller was actively suicidal, we were supposed to ask if we could contact emergency services and send help. But we weren't allowed to do that without the caller's permission. We also learned that most callers weren't actively suicidal but were calling because they were depressed and needed someone to talk to. In addition to the 24/7 phone line, Samaritans also offered a drop-in service that gave people a chance to have face-to-face meetings with a volunteer during business hours.

Every volunteer was expected to work one four-hour shift on the hotline each week, plus one overnight shift (from midnight to 8 a.m.) each month. These shifts took place at the Boston headquarters of Samaritans, Inc., on the second floor of an old, run-down building in Kenmore Square. The call center was a small room with desks and phones for up to four volunteers. With rare exceptions, there were at least two on duty at all times. Which I was relieved to hear.

It wasn't easy work. But I learned a lot, not only about myself, but also about the tremendous need out there for mental health services. Although we were doing our best to meet that need, there was just so much my fellow volunteers and I could do.

A few experiences stand out.

My usual shift was Sunday from 8 p.m. until midnight, but I once worked a shift during weekday hours, which led to my only opportunity to meet with a drop-in visitor. He walked into the Samaritans office and asked if he could speak with someone. Since I was the only volunteer available, I got the assignment. After I introduced myself and brought him to a small interview room, I asked how I could help.

He was about fifty years old and clearly down on his luck. His face was covered with stubble, his denim jacket was patched and dirty, and his overall appearance was disheveled. He told me he'd been living in a homeless shelter for the past few weeks and was spending his daytime hours wandering the streets of Boston. When I asked if he was suicidal, he said, "No...not yet, anyway." He was sensitive and intelligent, and I could see he was ashamed of his current situation. "I used to have a job and an apartment," he said. "But I got laid off...then I got evicted...and now this." When I asked what was bothering him the most, he said, "It's the way people on the street won't even look at me. And when they do, they usually look disgusted." At that moment, I found myself looking at him with compassion and told him so. I also suggested that some of the people out there were probably looking at him the same way. He seemed to take that in and finally said, with a tear in his eye, "Maybe you're right. I'll try to remember that."

That felt like a small win. But the victories were rare. More often than not, I didn't know if I was being helpful. Like the time I took a call from a 15-year-old girl who'd just arrived in Boston from a far Western state. When I asked why she was here, she told me a harrowing story about being cast out of her fundamentalist Christian family because she was a "bad seed." When I asked her to say more, she said her father had been coming into her bedroom at night to stroke her hair and touch her body, which she didn't like. He also told her not to say anything about it. Then one day he got mad, said it was all her fault, and that the devil was inside her. The next day her parents gave her some money and told her to leave them and her younger siblings and never come back. So she took a bus to Boston, which she had heard was a nice place to live. I told her she hadn't done anything wrong and that it sounded to me like her father was the one who was behaving badly. When I asked if she was suicidal, she said no, but she didn't know where she was going to stay or what to do next. I offered to give her the numbers of some places that could help, but then I heard some voices in the background and before I could give her the numbers she said, "I gotta go now," and hung up.

I could only hope she'd call back.

On another Sunday night, I got a call from a man who said he wanted to die and had just taken an overdose of his medication. I tried to get more details, but he wouldn't provide any. Instead, he kept repeating that he was ready to leave this life and didn't want to be alone as he passed. I asked for his address so I could send help, but he said no, he just wanted to die. As his speech became more slurred, I kept asking if I could send help, and he continued to refuse. Then there were long periods of silence, punctuated only by the sounds of his breathing and occasional comments such as "I'm still here" from me. Eventually, he hung up the phone and I was left listening to a dial tone.

I just sat there for a while feeling sad and confused. Did he die that night? Or did he sleep it off and wake up the next morning with a renewed commitment to live? Or was the whole thing just a prank? I didn't think so. But I'll never know for sure. I talked to the other volunteer on duty that night, who said, "Gee, that's a tough one. Why don't you go take a break?" So I went out and took a quick walk around the block. And it helped – a little.

After a year as a Samaritans volunteer, I was still unclear about whether I was ready to go back to school and change careers. I felt I needed to move on and try a different type of volunteer work, one that would give me a chance to develop longer-term relationships with people than I could during brief phone conversations with strangers. So I volunteered with a hospice organization and learned how to support people who were in the process of dying.

Some of the motivation to take on this next challenge came from my interest in Buddhism. I'd heard tales of Tibetan Buddhist monks who meditate in the charnel grounds, places where bodies of the dead are left to decompose and be preyed upon by worms, vultures, wild dogs, and other scavengers. I was also familiar with the Five Remembrances, a Buddhist teaching designed to help people accept the fact that we're all destined to die. It's said that bringing these "remembrances" to mind can help us live our lives more fully:

1. I am of the nature to grow old. There is no way to escape growing old.
2. I am of the nature to become sick. There is no way to escape becoming sick.
3. I am of the nature to die. There is no way to escape death.
4. All that is dear to me and everyone I love are of the nature to change. There is no way to escape being separated from them.
5. My actions are my only true belongings. I cannot escape the consequences of my actions. My actions are the ground on which I stand.

While these statements may seem morbid, they're designed to help us appreciate our lives and see the truth of our predicament more clearly: That everything in this world, including ourselves, is impermanent. Try as we might to accumulate wealth, status and good health, there's nothing we can ultimately hold on to. Instead of being morbid, these truths can help us understand the preciousness of life and keep our attention focused on the present moment. Because right now is the only time we can experience the magic of being alive.

What better way to come face-to-face with this teaching than by becoming a hospice volunteer?

So I contacted a hospice organization and went through another training program. Among other things, I learned I'd be part of a team that included doctors, nurses, social workers, physical and occupational therapists, pastoral counselors, and home health aides. And that if a patient's family requested a volunteer, the volunteer could be asked to work with the family in a variety of ways, usually by offering companionship to the patient or assisting the patient's primary caregiver.

My first case involved a woman in her eighties who was dying of cancer. Betty was a retired nurse and was one of the first African American nurses to work at a major Boston hospital. She was now living with her younger sister, who worked during the day and requested the services of a volunteer. My first order of business was meeting Betty and finding out how I could help. She was delighted to see me when I came to her apartment, and she told me that what she wanted more than anything was to go on a field trip.

"I haven't been outside in over two months!" she told me.

The only problem was, she was too weak to take more than a few shaky steps, leaning on her walker, from one room to another within her apartment. This was a problem I could solve. I told Betty I'd arrange to get her a wheelchair, deliver it, and take her pretty much wherever she wanted. She said that would be wonderful.

The next week, I showed up with the wheelchair and asked her where she'd like to go.

"Let's just take a spin around the neighborhood," she said.

So she took a seat in the wheelchair, and I brought her down the elevator and into the outside world. It was a sparkling spring day, and lots of people were out and about. As we walked along, I realized that Betty was a well-known and well-loved figure in her neighborhood. Just about everyone we passed dropped what they were doing and wanted to stop and chat.

"Oh, Betty, it's so good to see you. It's been so long. How *are* you?"

"I'm fine, I'm fine. And how are *you*?"

There was much laughter, as well as a few tears. And over the next few weeks, Betty and I went on field trips to get ice cream, stroll through a local park, and sit in a playground to watch the children play. We never talked about death and dying or the Buddhist teachings or anything like that. But as I was helping her get into my car one morning after one of our outings, she turned to me, smiled and said, "You know, I realize that I'm dying, but in some ways, I feel like I'm just coming alive!"

Talk about being in the moment! Those words were just as moving and profound as anything I'd ever heard from a meditation teacher.

Another memorable – and heartbreaking – case involved Cary and Vincent, two young Haitian American boys. This was at the height of the AIDS epidemic, which was hitting the local Haitian community especially hard. The boys' father had died of AIDS a year earlier, and their mother now had the disease and was getting close to death herself. The boys were healthy, and their mother thought they could use a "big brother" like me. She also had a healthy daughter named Lucy, and a volunteer named Tracy was assigned to work with her. Being a white guy, not knowing much about Haitian culture, and not having much experience with kids, I felt nervous the first time I visited the family. But Cary and Vincent gave me a warm welcome, and clearly appreciated my presence. Once a week or so, we'd go to a movie, get some burgers at McDonald's, or maybe watch a ball game on TV. Sometimes we'd just hang out and I'd help them with their homework. Occasionally, we'd get together with Lucy and Tracy for an afternoon at the local bowling alley or a special occasion like a birthday party. After their mother succumbed to her illness, we met one last time to say goodbye before they went to live with relatives in another state.

When it was over, I had mixed emotions. I knew I'd been helpful, but at the same time, I had a nagging feeling that I could have done more. This feeling was exacerbated about a year later when I learned that Tracy had adopted the younger of the two boys. All I could think was, "Wow, now *that's* dedication!" I was humbled, and I wondered if I was doing this work because I truly wanted to help people and do something to make the world a better place, or because I just wanted to feel better about myself.

It's a question that persists to this day.

Other hospice experiences also caused me to question my motives. Like the time I was assigned to work with a well-known author who was dying of cancer. He was married, but his wife worked full time, and they were looking for a volunteer who could provide companionship during his long, lonely days. During our initial session, we hit it off, and he said he'd like to continue meeting with me. But before our second meeting could take place, he died. I was surprised and sad, but mostly I was disappointed that I wouldn't be able to hang out with this accomplished and respected man.

Brutus, my trusty inner critic, jumped at the chance to taunt me, *"Don't you see, you selfish bastard?"* he whispered. *"You're just in this for yourself!"*

Then there was the elderly gentleman with an inoperable brain tumor. He lived with his daughter, and she needed a volunteer to watch him while she ran errands or went to her own medical appointments. So I took on that role. But during my first visit, the man became agitated and started hitting me with his cane. Fortunately, he was quite weak, so I could deflect the blows, and I somehow managed to calm him down. When his daughter returned, I told her what happened, and she apologized. But when I told the director of volunteers at the hospice office, she was appalled, said this wasn't a safe situation for a volunteer, and assigned me to another case.

After three years as a hospice volunteer, I was grateful for the experience and knew I'd learned a lot, but I still wondered about my motives. Was I really committed to working in human services? Or did I just want to win the approval of a new set of friends and elders – the teachers and fellow meditators I was meeting in Dharma circles? I couldn't say for sure, and I remained undecided about whether I should walk away from my burgeoning business as a freelance copywriter to pursue an uncertain career as a psychotherapist.

Eventually, I concluded that I didn't need to change careers after all. Christine and I were building a network of mutual friends, not only from CIMC, but also from our new neighborhood and with some of our professional colleagues. We were fixing up our house, which needed a new kitchen, a new bath, and other updates. I continued my freelance copywriting and started teaming up with Jim Baker, an art director buddy who recently left his ad agency job to become a freelancer. At the same time, I was getting vicarious pleasure out of listening to Christine talk about her work as a therapist, and I enjoyed being able to support her by paying off her student loans and making her life a little easier than it used to be.

Yes, it was a good life. Even Larry Rosenberg, who founded CIMC and remained one of my mentors, assured me in one of our private interviews that there was nothing wrong with working in advertising, and that he knew many people from the business world who were serious practitioners of meditation, and whose donations made it possible for places like IMS and CIMC to exist.

So maybe, just maybe, I thought, I could be one of those people and continue on my current path: freelancing, meditating, volunteering, supporting worthy causes, and living with Christine in our cozy little house till death did us part.

Then, just as I was settling into this happily-ever-after life, a series of eye-opening events shook me out of my stupor and showed me that I still needed to make a major course correction.

CHAPTER FIFTEEN

Life is Short

I was sitting at home on a lazy Sunday morning in 1998 when the telephone rang. Alison, the wife of Jim Baker, my friend and fellow freelancer, was on the other end. And she was struggling to get the words out.

Alison, Jim and I all worked at the same ad agency back in the 1980s – the one that sent me on that TV shoot in New York. I didn't have much contact with Alison back then, but Jim's office was next to mine, and the two of us teamed up on a number of projects. We were both in the same profession, both about the same age, both single, and both on the look-out for female companionship. With all that in common, we became fast friends. After we both left the agency and began working together on freelance projects, I began to think of him as my best friend, a phrase that hadn't been part of my vocabulary since high school.

Back when all of us were still at the agency, Jim came into my office one day and said he wanted to talk. He was a big guy, about six-foot-four, and unlike me, he had a happy-go-lucky attitude toward life. Which was one of the reasons I enjoyed his company. But on this day, he seemed troubled. When I asked what was on his mind, he confessed that he had a major crush on Alison. But there was an obvious problem. She was married. And he wasn't sure what to do.

Well, I wasn't sure what to tell him. But based on my own experience with married women, I said he'd probably be better off if he looked elsewhere for a partner.

"Yeah, that's what I've been thinking," he said. "I'll just keep telling myself there's someone else like Alison out there for me, and all I have to do is find her."

Well, that was Jim's intention, and I believe he meant it. But things didn't quite work out according to plan. After a while, he told Alison how tough it was trying to meet someone out there, and she listened. Then she told him how painful it was being stuck in an unhappy marriage, and he listened. There was more talking and more listening, one thing led to another, and Alison eventually decided to leave her husband and marry Jim. And they were a happy couple. They bought a house just a few miles down the road from Christine and me, and they became part of our circle of friends. After a few years, they added a vacation home in Maine, which is where Alison was when she called me on that lazy Sunday morning.

"What's wrong, Alison?"

Interrupted by frequent and painful sobbing, she told me that Jim had died earlier that morning. She'd been working in the garden, and he was inside reading the paper. Then the quiet morning was interrupted by a crash from inside the house. She rushed in and found Jim lying on the floor next to the sofa, not breathing and unresponsive. She called 911 and tried giving him CPR, but by the time the ambulance arrived, he was gone. He was pronounced dead, apparently of a massive heart attack, at the local hospital in Maine.

Alison was in shock, and so was I. Jim had always seemed so robust and healthy. He loved his life. Then I remembered that he'd spent a night in the hospital for some tests a few months earlier because of an irregular heartbeat, but the doctors told him everything looked OK and there was nothing to worry about.

After the funeral, something shifted in my mind and heart. I'd lost my best friend and a close professional colleague. And while I was grieving his loss, I couldn't help but realize on a deeper level than ever before that I, too, could die at any time. Jim had just turned 50. I was about to turn 45. How much time did I have left? Of course, I didn't know. But I did know that how I intended to use that time was important. And if I wanted to use it doing something other than coming up with a bunch of clever advertising slogans, I'd better act soon.

Around that same time, I was thinking about the *kilesas* – or torments of the mind – which according to Buddhism are the basic causes of human suffering. These three powerful forces are greed, hatred, and delusion. Greed is the tendency of the mind to cling to pleasant experiences. Hatred is the related tendency to push away unpleasant experiences. Delusion is the mind's tendency to become lost, confused, and not see things clearly. Together, these forces cause us to cling to the pleasant, avoid the unpleasant, and, in our confusion, not see clearly that all experiences in this world are impermanent and can never bring lasting happiness. By not living in harmony with this truth, we create unnecessary suffering in our lives.

According to Buddhist teachings, by practicing meditation and paying close attention to how the mind reacts to the endless barrage of pleasant and unpleasant experiences we're all faced with every day, we can slowly weaken the *kilesas* until we become free of them and reach enlightenment, the sublime state in which the *kilesas* are totally extinguished.

As I thought about this, I began to see one of the central conflicts in my life in a new way: I was spending hundreds of hours each year

on a meditation cushion attempting to weaken and eventually up-
root the forces of greed, hatred, and delusion. But at the same time, I
was spending even more hours creating clever advertising messages
designed to fertilize, water, and encourage those very same forces to
grow – in myself as well as in the readers, listeners, and viewers of the
ads I was creating.

When I saw this contradiction, I started to laugh. But then I realized that in addition to being funny, it was a big reason why I wasn't
satisfied with my chosen profession. And I knew I had to do something about it.

Shortly after this, I took a class at CIMC on Wise Speech led by
Narayan Liebenson. Wise Speech is part of Buddhism's Noble Eightfold Path, which also includes Wise View, Wise Thought, Wise Action,
Wise Livelihood, Wise Effort, Wise Mindfulness, and Wise Concen-
tration. The Buddha taught that this path, when followed faithfully
to its end, leads to enlightenment, to the end of suffering, and to the
deepest levels wisdom and compassion.

In her class, Narayan talked about various aspects of Wise Speech.
She said it's primarily about practicing speech that is kind, true, helpful, and necessary – as well as avoiding speech that is harsh, false,
divisive, and unnecessary. All this was familiar to me. But then she
added something that really got my attention. She said Wise Speech
also means avoiding speech that attempts to present things "in a certain way." This is speech that doesn't tell the whole truth. It's speech
that contains at least a dash of propaganda, that has an agenda, that's
intended to produce a certain result, a result that may not be in the
listener's best interest.

When I heard this, I instantly thought, "Oh my God, that's what I
do for a living." And it was true. I was spending all my working hours
creating advertising messages designed to present my clients' prod-

ucts and services in a certain way. The words I was crafting weren't false – the FTC has laws against that – but they didn't tell the whole truth and nothing but the truth. They had an agenda. They were intended to motivate people to make a purchase, a purchase that may or may not be in their best interest.

Once again, I saw a conflict between what I aspired to in my spiritual life and what I was doing in my professional life.

Another lightning bolt hit me while I was writing a series of radio and TV commercials for a chain of carpet stores. This was a big project, and it paid well. But it was a real grind. Day after day, I was getting input from the client, coming up with ideas for the campaign, then writing the copy, presenting it to the client, getting feedback, rewriting the copy, trying to get all the right words into the thirty- and sixty-second spots. One evening in the middle of this project Christine came home and cheerfully asked, "How was your day?"

"Terrible," I said. "I spent another whole day writing ads about storewide carpet sales!"

Suddenly I realized in a new way that in addition to the ethical dilemmas involved with my work, it was something I just didn't want to do any more.

But did I have the guts to walk away? Not quite yet. My doubts and fears persisted. So I decided to go back into therapy. Jonathan, my former therapist, wasn't available. So I reached out to Richard, a therapist who specialized in treating anxiety, for I believed that anxiety was the only thing preventing me from making the changes I wanted to make in my life. And Richard was helpful. He taught me strategies to reduce anxiety by changing my inner talk and transforming its messages of fear and failure into messages of hope and possibility. In the process, he helped me see Brutus – the inner critic who sat on my shoulder and slugged me on the side of the head every time I was about to take a chance and risk making a mistake – in a different way. Richard suggested that instead of a sadist who took pleasure in torturing me, I could think of him as an "anxious chatterbox," a chronic worrywart who was, in his own misguided way, trying to help me. Instead of being afraid of him or fighting with him, I could ask him to calm down and consider that underneath all the inflammatory rhetoric, he might have something to say that's worth listening to. This made him much easier to get along with.

Richard also asked me to create a graphic "lifeline" depicting the major milestones in my life up to that point as well as the milestones I hoped to reach in the future. Through that exercise, it became clear that the most important thing I still hoped to do was go back to school and become a psychotherapist.

The clincher came one day when I returned home after a therapy session and saw a magnet on our refrigerator, one I hadn't noticed in a long time. It featured a quotation attributed to Gandhi that said, "Be the change you wish to see in the world."

Finally, I gave myself permission to be that change.

PART THREE

Wide Awake

CHAPTER SIXTEEN

Taking the Leap

It was time to act. But first, I wanted to be sure Christine was on board. So after dinner one night, as we sat at the table finishing a shared glass of wine, I looked at her and said, in as serious a tone as I could muster, "Can I ask you something?"

"Of course," she said, looking concerned.

"Well, I've been talking with Richard about what I want to do with the rest of my life, and the idea of going back to school and becoming a therapist keeps coming up."

"Oh, is that all?" she said, sounding relieved. "So you're finally gonna do it?"

"We've got more than enough saved to cover the tuition," I added, "but we'll have to cut back on our expenses while I'm in school."

"That's OK."

"Which means no more fancy vacations, at least for a while," I continued, "and no more going out to dinner every time we feel like it."

"No problem."

"And I think we should let our house cleaner go."

"We can do it ourselves on the weekends."

"Are you sure you're OK, with this?"

"Honey, your work has been making you miserable. I'm *glad* you're finally ready to make a change."

"Even if it means living a more frugal life?"

"Remember, I was barely able to make ends meet before I met you. We'll still be better off than I was back then. I'm not worried at all. And I think you'll make a very good therapist."

I was pleased but not surprised that she was so supportive. But I was still worried she might have trouble adjusting to our new austerity measures. Then, a few days later, she proved just how fully on board she was when we were shopping at Trader Joe's. When I plopped a big box of nectarines into our cart, she looked at me disapprovingly. "Put 'em back," she said. "They're not in season, and they're way too expensive." I didn't agree, but I took it as proof she was ready to economize and complied with her request.

A few weeks later, I signed up for that developmental psychology course at Lesley University, after which Christine convinced me that instead of a Master's in Counseling Psychology, I'd be better off with a Master's in Social Work.

So I looked into local social work schools and requested an application to the MSW program at Simmons University in Boston, which made my plan to change careers feel much more real. But going through the application process – completing the forms, taking the standardized tests, seeking letters of recommendation, being interviewed – felt strange. It was something I hadn't gone through in nearly 25 years. And the strangeness triggered my simmering doubts and fears. But my fears subsided a bit when I showed up at Simmons for my interview and bumped into a woman I had worked with at one of those Boston ad agencies years before.

"What are you doing here, Tom?" she asked with a surprised look on her face.

"Well, believe it or not, I'm applying to become a full-time student in the MSW program."

"Good for you!" she said. "I got my MSW here last year and it's the best thing I've ever done."

So maybe my plan wasn't so strange after all. This time, instead of listening to my fears or fighting with them, I just let them be. This time, I was committed to continue walking down this path I'd chosen until I either reached my goal or it became absolutely clear I was making a mistake.

My application to Simmons was accepted, and I began the two-year MSW program there in the fall of 1999. Being back in school was a refreshing change, although it continued to feel strange. I was a middle-aged man, and most of my classmates were much younger women. This was not unexpected. Social work has always been a profession dominated by women, which is one of the reasons why social workers' salaries are so low. Unfortunately, despite the movement toward gender equality over the past century, we still live in a patriarchal society. Men still dominate the ranks of CEOs, corporate boards, university presidents, and the halls of Congress. On top of that, our system of capitalism places a high value on work that contributes to economic growth, such as manufacturing, high technology, financial services, and yes, even advertising and marketing. It also assigns a significantly lower value to work in education, human services, and health care, especially in those health care professions – such as nursing, mental health, and social work – where women are in the majority.

All this continues to change in what I consider to be the right direction. But it's going to take time for true justice and equality to reign. Maybe a lot of time. And as I was reminded when my friend Jim died so suddenly, our time on this planet is limited. I knew in a more visceral way than ever before that if I wanted to make a change in my life, I couldn't just sit around and wait for conditions to improve.

Once classes started, that feeling of strangeness morphed into a sense of connection. Within a month or two, I knew I was surrounded by like-minded people. My classmates and teachers at Simmons were politically progressive, were working to create a more egalitarian society, and were helping others make the most of their lives in the meantime. I also knew I was in a supportive setting – an environment that was more cooperative than competitive, where people cared more about each other than about getting to the head of the class.

It was similar to the way I felt when I graduated from college and started the Master of Arts in Teaching program at Northwestern.

It was also similar to the way I felt at the local meditation center. It was the kind of feeling I wanted to experience more often in my life – especially in my professional life. And it was very different from the way I felt when I was working in advertising. Or even when I was in college. Back then, I not only felt the competitiveness all around me, but also felt like I was just drifting. I didn't know which courses to take or what to major in, because I had no idea what I wanted to do with my life. Plus, my parents were footing the bill. So I was free to float along, taking whatever classes I felt like taking, without having to think too much about where it was leading or what the cost might be. Now, since I had a sense of direction – and since I was paying my own way – it was much easier for me to appreciate the value of my education. It was also easier to know which courses were relevant to my goals and therefore, which ones to sign up for. As best I could, I made sure everything I was learning was preparing me to be an effective mental health clinician.

In addition to my work in the classroom, I was spending a significant amount of time in the field, getting experience as a social work intern in real-world mental health settings. Each week during our two years in the MSW program, my classmates and I spent three full days in hospitals, community mental health centers, public schools, and other professional settings throughout the Boston area, where we worked directly with clients and were supervised by experienced social workers. Then we got together on campus the other two days to attend classes. This was a great way to learn about theory and methods and at the same time have opportunities to put those theories and methods – as well as ourselves – to the test in the field.

My first-year field placement was in an adult day treatment program, a program designed to help people with serious psychiatric disorders manage their illnesses and stay out of the hospital. These programs were created, not coincidentally, at the same time most of the big, state-run psychiatric hospitals – more commonly known as insane asylums – were being shut down. This process of "deinstitutionalization" began in 1955 with the introduction of Thorazine, the first effective anti-psychotic drug, and it accelerated during the '60s and '70s as more new medications were introduced.

Some of the reasons behind the deinstitutionalization movement were altruistic. Most of the state psychiatric hospitals were basically warehouses for people with serious mental illnesses such as schizophrenia, bipolar disorder, and severe depression, as well as developmental disorders such as autism and Down syndrome. Once they were committed to such a hospital, usually against their will, these unfortunate souls were often condemned to spend the rest of their lives there, enduring conditions that were sometimes neglectful and even abusive. The deinstitutionalization movement sought to change this by recognizing that people with serious mental illnesses and developmental disorders have civil rights like every other citizen. It helped them have more freedom and integrate them into society –

not only through the use of effective medications, but also by transferring their care from the state-run hospitals to a network of newly created, federally funded community mental health centers.

But there was another, more practical reason why so many people were deinstitutionalized, and it was all about the money. As the nationwide population of the big psychiatric hospitals swelled to an all-time high of 559,000 in 1955, running and maintaining these facilities became extremely expensive. So the mass transfer began. By 1994, that population was down to just 72,000. Most of the big state hospitals were permanently closed. And most of the patients who had lived in one, or would have been sent to one, were being treated on an outpatient basis at community mental health centers.

The adult day treatment program I was assigned to was in one of those centers. It was the Tri-City Mental Health Center in Lynn, Massachusetts, a city about 12 miles north of Boston where a struggling working class makes up a significant portion of the population. When I arrived there in the fall of 1999, Tri-City Mental Health Center was also struggling to survive. That's because much of the federal funding for community mental health centers, which began to flow when President Kennedy signed the Community Mental Health Centers Construction Act in 1963, had been cut. These cuts deepened during the 1980s, when President Reagan boldly declared, "Government is not the *solution* to our problem, government *is* the problem." Inspired by these words, the budget hawks in Washington went on a crusade to end the era of "big government." Then, during the 1990s, many state legislatures followed suit by "privatizing" services that had formerly been provided by the government, including mental health care.

I didn't know any of this when I drove up to the Tri-City Mental Health Center for my first day as a social work intern in the fall of 1999. All I knew was that my late-model Volvo looked conspicuously more upscale than the other cars in the parking lot, including the one owned by the program's clinical director. I was also struck by the down-and-out – and in some cases, "out-of-it" – appearance of the clients gathered outside the entrance to the building. Most of them were smoking and chatting with each other. But one young man was standing off to the side, talking to himself, or perhaps to the voices in his head. And one older woman was off to the other side, pacing back and forth in a determined, purposeful way. These were people who probably would have been committed to a state psychiatric hospital back in the 1950s. They were also the people I'd be working with for the next nine months.

My heart started racing as I approached them. They got quiet, and I could feel their eyes on me as I walked past them and into the building. I could also feel my anxiety level hitting 9.5 on a 10-point scale. Was I ready for this? I didn't really know, but I was ready to find out.

CHAPTER SEVENTEEN

Entering the Arena

As it turned out, my fears were highly exaggerated.

The clients in the Tri-City adult day treatment program made me – and Rachel, the other social work intern from Simmons – feel welcome right from the start. It was clear to us that many of them were not only happy to receive regular attention from two new clinicians-in-training, but also proud to play a part in that training.

But there were notable exceptions. Every week or two, someone would test us, either intentionally or unintentionally, which gave us a chance to show what we were made of. Or not. This was part of our training, too. I got my first taste of this in a group I was assigned to co-lead with Alan, a clinician on the Tri-City staff. His "Substance Use and Abuse" group met once a week and was for people struggling with addictions. Before introducing me to the group, Alan sat down with me in his office, told me that our goals included helping members stay clean and sober, remaining supportive if and when they relapsed, and giving them a place where they could discuss their challenges and support each other. He also told me a little about each group member, and he advised me to take it slow and just observe things during my first meeting, which was about to begin.

"That sounds good to me," I say as we leave his office and walk toward the group room.

When we enter, I see a desk in the corner and eight chairs arranged in a circle at the center of the windowless room. Seven of the chairs are occupied by clients, some of whom are chatting with each other, and one chair is empty. I sit in the empty chair while Alan grabs the desk chair and joins the circle. I notice the institutional gray carpet on the floor and the lack of decoration on the walls. I also notice that five of the clients are men and two are women, that the youngest looks like he's barely out of high school while the oldest is probably in his seventies, and that they all look like they've been through hard times.

"OK, everyone," says Alan as he clears his throat, looks around the room, and waits for everyone to quiet down. When they do, he adds, "Now I know most of you met Tom in today's opening meeting. But for those who didn't, this is Tom Pedulla, a social work intern from Simmons, and he'll be part of this group until next spring."

Two or three members say "Welcome, Tom" or "Hi, Tom" or just "Hey."

I look around, nod at those who spoke, and say, "Thanks for letting me be part of this group."

Again, a few members mumble, "Sure," "No problem," or "We're glad to have you."

Then the room gets quiet until Alan asks, "So who wants to start things off today?"

The silence continues for at least a full minute. Then a large, surly looking woman wearing sweatpants and a fleece pullover raises her hand and says, "Wait a second! Before we get started, I wanna ask the new guy something."

After another pause, Alan says, "OK, Barbara, go ahead," while I feel like a deer in the headlights and wonder what the heck I'm going to say to whatever it is she's going to ask me.

"I just want to know," she says as she stares intensely at me, "if *you've* ever had a problem with drugs or booze. Because if you've never been an addict, then you don't belong in this group."

Oh, boy, I wonder to myself, *how am I supposed to answer that one?* Although I sometimes overindulged when I was in college and in the ad biz, I've never had a problem with alcohol or drugs. However, through my work as a psychotherapy client, I've come to see myself as addicted to seeking approval. In my meditation practice, I've also learned that I'm more-or-less addicted to worrying. So I take a breath and say, "Well, Barbara, like most of the staff here, I don't want to get into my personal history. But in my opinion, just about everyone in this world is or has been addicted to something."

I'm not sure how she felt about my answer, but she seemed satisfied and never asked me about it again, so I guess I passed the test.

Later, Alan apologized for putting me on the spot and said I handled it well. He and the rest of the staff at Tri-City took their roles as mentors seriously. And like the clients at Tri-City, they also seemed pleased to have two new interns on board. After all, we were there to help lighten their load as well as to learn from them.

Each day, the program began with socializing for the clients – which is what the folks hanging around outside the building were doing when I first arrived – and a brief staff meeting in the clinical director's office for the rest of us. During these meetings we'd hear about any new clients who were being admitted to the program, and each of us would have a chance to tell the team about any concerns we had about the clients we were working with individually. Then, at 9:30, the clients and staff would gather in the dining room for the opening meeting. This was led by the clinical director, who took at-tendance, read the daily announcements, introduced any new clients (or staff members), and gave the clients a chance to ask questions or make any announcements they wanted to share with the community. The rest of the day went something like this:

10-11:30AM	Group therapy sessions led by various staff members
11:30-Noon	Lunch prep for some, individual meetings with case coordinators for others
12-12:30PM	Lunch
12:30-1PM	Lunch clean-up for some, individual meetings with case coordinators for others
1-2:30PM	Group therapy sessions led by various staff members
2:30-3PM	Closing meeting, clients dismissed
3-5PM	Time for staff to complete paperwork, make phone calls, coordinate client care with outside providers

At Tri-City, as in most adult day treatment programs, the primary mode of treatment was group therapy, and the menu of choices was extensive. It included psychotherapy groups, where clients were free to talk about whatever was on their minds, as well as groups that were focused on particular topics, such art therapy, relapse prevention, music appreciation, social skills, self-esteem, symptom management, spirituality, current events, women's issues, men's issues, and more.

When these programs were created, they were designed to be a less restrictive, more compassionate, and less expensive holding envi-ronment than the locked wards in the state-run psychiatric hospitals. The term "holding environment" was coined by the British psycho-analyst D. W. Winnicott, who believed that successful mental health treatment requires the creation of an environment where clients feel safely held emotionally, similar to the way infants feel safely held physically by sensitive, caring parents. In the early days of adult day treatment, clients were usually free to stay in these programs as long as they wanted or needed to, which helped foster this feeling of being safely held.

But by the time I arrived on the scene, things had changed. Because of budget cuts that began in the 1980s, state-funded Medicaid and other managed care insurance plans were pressuring the administrators of day treatment programs to treat clients for a limited amount of time – anywhere from a few weeks to a few months – and to focus on helping clients get their lives back on track so they could "graduate" from the program. Occasionally this could happen, especially if the client had a life to get back to. But the vast majority of the clients at Tri-City were in the program for many months or even years. Most of them were unable to work because of their psychiatric disabilities, and most didn't have families who could take care of them. So the day treatment program became their surrogate family as well as their extended community. In a beautiful way, it became a place where they could connect with others, give and receive support, celebrate holidays, and grieve losses together. But unfortunately, since the possibility of a sudden and unwanted discharge was hanging over their heads, the environment was not as safe or secure as it could have been.

Still, the program had much to offer. In addition to the group meetings that were its backbone, it provided individual case coordinators for each client. Besides running the groups, every full-time clinician served as the case coordinator for about seven clients. As part-time interns, Rachel and I were asked to cover just two. We met individually with each of these clients once a week to ask how things were going, both in the day treatment program and in their outside lives. We also coordinated their care with their individual therapists and other outside providers. My two clients were Diana, a woman in her thirties with bipolar disorder and type 1 diabetes, and Ray, a man in his twenties with schizophrenia who had recently been arrested for assaulting a woman in a donut shop.

As interns, we were also group co-leaders, which meant working with different staff members in their groups, observing them in action and learning from their different styles. After an initial orientation period, we were encouraged to participate more and more in the group interactions, and we were eventually given opportunities to take the lead, at least occasionally. In fact, when one full-time staffer left her job halfway through the year, I was asked to lead the meditation group she had started, a job I was happy to take on.

Integrating meditation with my work life was one of the reasons I wanted to change careers in the first place. Of course, I could always do my best to be mindful whenever I was working. But in addition to practicing mindfulness myself, I also wanted to share some of the meditation techniques that had been helpful to me with others. The meditation group at Tri-City Mental Health Center was my first opportunity to do that. Since we were in a secular setting, I didn't talk about the Buddhist teachings or anything else that could be construed as religious. But I did show the group members how to slow down, sink below their thinking minds into their feeling bodies, and notice that, among other things, their bodies were breathing. This allowed them to let go of their troubled thoughts and painful emotions and simply breathe, if only for a few moments at a time. Which many of them found helpful. Like my predecessor, I also led guided meditations that invited clients to imagine themselves in beautiful, natural settings – a quiet beach, a mountaintop, a peaceful forest – and notice the sights, sounds and smells that surrounded them. Although not out of the traditional Buddhist playbook, this kind of visualization was another way to help clients relax and take a break from their busy schedules and even busier minds.

Serving as case coordinator for Diana and Ray presented another set of challenges and opportunities. On the opportunity side, it gave me a chance to experience what it would be like to work as an individual psychotherapist, which was my ultimate goal. On the challenging side, it was the first time I'd be working one-on-one with people who were struggling with serious mental illnesses. I'd be on my own, with no co-leaders or other group members to back me up, help me out, or defuse any tension that might be building in the room.

Diana turned out to be easy to work with. She was generally upbeat and engaged in our meetings. She was also willing to consider any feedback I had to offer. The only challenging situation I remember occurred one day when I noticed she was more talkative than usual in her morning group. Later that day, when we were meeting one-on-one, she was even more revved up, talking and laughing about all kinds of things, and giving me few opportunities to interrupt. I suspected she'd stopped taking her mood stabilizing medication and was in a hypomanic state. If left unchecked, this could turn into a full-blown manic episode, which could lead to hospitalization. So when she finally took a breath, I took a chance and asked the question that needed to be asked:

"Diana, are you still taking all your medications as prescribed?"

This can be a risky question since clients often respond to it defensively with denial and anger. But Diana just stopped and wanted to know why I was asking. So I described the behavior I'd been observing, both in the morning group and in our current meeting, and said I was concerned she was getting manic and could end up in the hospital as a result.

She blushed and admitted she'd stopped taking her mood stabilizer. Then she asked if she was in trouble. I assured her that she wasn't in trouble at all, that I was glad she told me, but that I needed to tell her psychiatrist and she needed follow his instructions. Which she promised to do. When I saw her again the following week, she was much calmer and more coherent. She told me she was back on the medication and thanked me for noticing the change in her behavior.

My other individual client was Ray, and he presented a different set of challenges. He was awaiting trial for his attack on the woman in the donut shop, which involved a knife, resulted in injuries to the woman, and was of grave concern to Ray's family, the victim and her family, and the community at large. Ray was diagnosed with paranoid schizophrenia, and although he was taking antipsychotic medications, some of his delusions and paranoid thinking persisted. In our first few meetings, I focused on getting to know him and building a sense of mutual trust, or as it's known in the field, a therapeutic alliance. This wasn't an easy task. Ray was suspicious of me and reluctant to share information about himself and his inner world. Eventually, I asked about the assault in the donut shop. He said he didn't know the woman, but that a voice in his head told him she was evil and had to be stopped. When I asked him if he still felt that way, he said no. But there was an emptiness in his eyes and a lack of expression in his voice that made it hard to know what he was really thinking and feeling. And how was I feeling? Anxious. Out of my depth. I didn't look forward to meeting with him because I often didn't know what to say or how to connect. I'm afraid I didn't make much progress with him during the course of the year, and when I left the program in May, his trial was still pending. I never found out what happened to Ray. And to this day, he remains one of the most alarming and enigmatic clients I've ever worked with.

Of course, my old friend Brutus, who was always ready to attack whenever I made a mistake, was still on duty. And as a first-year intern in a place like Tri-City Mental Health Center, I made my share of mistakes. But by this time, I had another technique I could use to soften Brutus's blows. It was something I'd learned at a nine-day metta retreat at the Insight Meditation Society.

Metta is a Pali word that's usually translated as *lovingkindness*. It's the natural tendency of the heart to wish ourselves and others well. And while it may be natural, it's often obscured by negative forces in the mind and heart, afflictive emotions such as fear, anger, envy, selfishness, and confusion. But it can be awakened and strengthened by practicing metta meditation, which is what I did for nine straight days and nights at the metta retreat.

Metta meditation involves silently repeating certain phrases designed to cultivate feelings of lovingkindness. There are many different traditional phrases to choose from, and practitioners are encouraged to create their own as well. We're also advised not to practice with more than three or four at a time.

Some of my personal favorites are:

May I be safe and protected from inner and outer harm.
May I be peaceful.
May I be free from suffering.
May I be fully at ease.

When I learned about this practice, I was taught to send lovingkindness first to myself, then to send it out to others, starting with a benefactor, someone who had helped or inspired me. To do that, all I had to do was think of that person and change the pronoun to "you":

May you be safe and protected from inner and outer harm.
May you be peaceful.
May you be free from suffering.
May you be fully at ease.

After that, I was instructed to move through a series of other people, progressing from the easiest to the most challenging: a dear friend, a neutral person (someone I didn't know well and didn't have strong feelings about), then a difficult person (someone who had harmed me or who just annoys me). Finally, I was asked to send lovingkindness to all beings, including myself, including all the people described above, all the people on Earth, all the animals and other non-human beings with whom we share this planet, and all beings everywhere, those seen and unseen, known and unknown, throughout the vast reaches of the universe and any other possible dimensions of existence.

> *May all beings be safe and protected from inner and outer harm.*
> *May all beings be peaceful.*
> *May all beings be free from suffering.*
> *May all beings be fully at ease.*

Lovingkindness practice can be done for a few minutes at the start or end of a meditation period, or pretty much any other time – while walking down the street, meeting with a client, watching the news on TV, having a difficult discussion with a loved one. In fact, it can be especially helpful to bring these phrases to mind and to wish oneself and others well when in the midst of conflict.

When I signed up for the metta retreat, I knew my fellow yogis and I would be expected to practice lovingkindness all day long – while sitting, walking, eating, getting ready for bed, taking a shower, even while sitting on the toilet. It was designed to be a totally immersive experience. And it turned out to be transformative.

One of the biggest things it transformed was my relationship with Brutus. Yes, he continued to show up, even on a lovingkindness retreat, because of course, I continued to make mistakes. I'd take too much food at lunch. Or say something stupid during a private meeting with one of the teachers. Or make eye contact with an attractive woman that caused her to look away. As soon as I made the slightest misstep, Brutus would appear on my shoulder and start swinging his hammer. But for the first time, I realized that instead of taking sadistic pleasure in beating me up, he wasn't enjoying himself in the slightest. In fact, I could see that he hated his job, but felt he had to do it in order to make me a better, more likable human being. And suddenly, for the first time, I saw him with lovingkindness and compassion. So I told him he could stop, that it was OK, that *I* was OK, and that he could relax and let us both be exactly the way we are, with all our imperfections intact.

This was during a nine-day period when I was practicing intensively, and the ceasefire didn't last. When I returned home, Brutus was back. But something had changed. He wasn't quite as nasty as he'd been before. And I knew that instead of trying to fight with him or get rid of him, I could meet him with lovingkindness and compassion.

Or at least I could try.

CHAPTER EIGHTEEN

Becoming a Therapist

It's October of 2000. I'm in my second year of social work school, and my field placement is in the outpatient psychiatry department at Cambridge Health Alliance. I've just introduced myself to Frank, one of my first clients, and I'm leading him from the waiting room to the office where we'll begin our work together. I'm nervous but trying not to let it show. The office we're heading for is tiny, just big enough for a student-sized desk and two chairs – one for me and one for Frank. There's a small pot of African violets on the windowsill and a ticking clock on the wall, along with an unframed print of Monet's "Garden at Giverny," which is held up by colored pushpins. Although I'm starting to think of this as "my" office, it's a room I share with several other trainees and well as some part-time senior clinicians.

Frank is about my age and height, but he's stockier and more power-fully built. He looks like he's spent some serious time lifting weights. He has dark wavy hair, olive skin, and is wearing jeans and a Ralph Lauren polo shirt. As we walk down the hall, I notice he's carrying a paper bag. When we reach the office, I show him in, close the door, and ask him to take a seat. Before doing so, he reaches into the bag, pulls out a plastic produce bag containing a large bunch of green grapes, and plops it down on the desk. He looks at me, smiles and says, "These are for you."

Oh, no, I think. *What am I supposed to do now?*

Although this is our first meeting, I already know something about Frank from reading the summary of his intake session, which was conducted by a senior clinician. According to the intake, Frank was convicted of distributing narcotics and was recently released from federal prison after serving three years of a five-year sentence. He's seeking therapy because it's one of the conditions of his parole, but he claims it's also because he wants to change his life. He's living with his older brother in Boston and wants to find a job so he can move out and get his own place. He says he's committed to staying away from drugs, because in addition to selling narcotics, he started using and became addicted to them. This, he believes, was the start of his downfall. He got sloppy with his business dealings and was nabbed by the DEA. While incarcerated, he joined a 12-step program, and he claims he's been clean and sober for the past three years – which were spent behind bars – and he wants to stay that way. But he knows the temptations of the outside world will present him with some challenges.

And he's just presented one to me.

As I look at this beautiful bunch of grapes on my desk, I wonder how to respond. On the one hand, I've been told I'm not supposed to accept gifts from clients. That was the policy at Tri-City Mental Health Center, and it's the policy at Cambridge Health Alliance. In social work school, I've been repeatedly reminded about the importance of maintaining professional boundaries between myself and my clients, and I was taught that accepting gifts from clients is a violation of those boundaries. But I know there are exceptions, especially if the gift is a small one. I also know Frank is an Italian American, as I am, and that an offering of food is a common and important part of our shared heritage. I don't want to hurt his feelings, but I also don't want to set a bad precedent. After quickly weighing all these factors and knowing that Frank has recently served time in prison for violating the law, I decide it's best to avoid any boundary violations in our relationship. So I play this one by the book.

"Gee, that's very thoughtful of you, Frank, and they look delicious. But I'm afraid I'm not allowed to accept gifts from clients."

"Oh, c'mon...take 'em! Who's gonna know?"

"Well, you'll know. And I'll know. So I appreciate the gesture, but I'll feel better if you bring them home and share them with someone else, OK?"

"Well, OK, if you say so."

It was an awkward start to our relationship. And I wasn't sure I did the right thing.

There were several reasons why I chose Cambridge Health Alliance for my field placement during my final year of social work school. As an affiliate of Harvard Medical School, CHA had an excellent reputation for training mental health professionals of all stripes. It was also a place where I'd get solid experience doing one-on-one psychotherapy. And it was recommended to me by Christine, who was a clinical social worker in CHA's outpatient geriatric service at the time.

As part of the public health system, CHA serves some of the region's poorest clients, including recent immigrants from Central and South America, the Caribbean, the Middle East, Asia, Africa, and Europe. Because of its proximity to Harvard, MIT, and Tufts, it also treats students and staff from those prestigious universities. The diversity of the communities it serves offers a rich learning environment for social work interns and other trainees.

During my nine months as a CHA intern, I was on a team that included many senior clinicians – psychiatrists, psychologists, social workers, clinical nurse specialists – and other student interns like myself. My team, the Wednesday Team, met every Wednesday morning for two hours to discuss new patients and decide which clinicians would be assigned to work with them. This was also a good time for interns to bring up any questions we had about our clients.

The team meetings were just one place where I could ask questions. I also met once a week with a veteran social worker who'd been seeing patients at CHA for many years and had a small private practice on the side. These weekly, hour-long supervision sessions were a huge help. In addition, all the social work interns met as a group with the head of CHA's social work department every Friday to share our concerns and discuss various aspects of our work. Once a week, there was yet another meeting in which all the interns – social workers-, psychologists- and psychiatrists-to-be – got together to hear a senior clinician present a case. As the year went on, we were also given opportunities to present cases of our own.

It was a setting where much was given, and much was expected. Not surprisingly, I sometimes felt like an impostor, especially when I looked around at the other interns, most of whom were younger, female, and deeply committed to their work. I figured most of them had known they wanted to pursue a career in the helping professions since they were in high school. As anxiety and self-doubt arose in my mind, right on cue, Brutus weighed in with his negative commentary: *Are you sure you belong here? I don't think you've got what it takes. These other trainees seem much more dedicated, confident, and qualified than you.*

But Brutus wasn't as brutal as he used to be. For I knew he was simply expressing my own insecurities, worries, and misgivings. So I thanked him for his concerns and, as Larry Rosenberg advised in that meditation retreat a decade earlier, I stuck with the mind that brought me there.

A few weeks after meeting Frank, I introduced myself to Jade, another interesting and challenging client. I was struck by the intensity in her eyes, the colorful tattoos on her arms, and her dark hair, which was cropped short and dyed pink on one side. She told me she was born during the final days of a hippie commune in northern California. Her mother was an Asian American artist and peace activist, and her father was an African American poet and musician. When the commune broke up, her parents, who never married, did the same. Her father stayed on the West Coast, and her mother moved with young Jade to the Boston area. After graduating from high school, Jade became the lead singer in a rock band with a small but loyal following. And she was still dreaming of making it big in the music business. But the band's popularity had waned over the past few years, and Jade was starting to feel her dreams slip away. She was also feeling anxious and drinking more than she used to. Which is why her mother begged her to see a therapist, an idea Jade fought against but eventually agreed to try. "Mostly to shut my mother up," she said. Our first session went fairly well, or so I thought. But after that, things went downhill fast.

I'm sitting in my office, waiting for Jade to show up for our second session. Fifteen minutes after the appointed time, I hear a knock on the door. After I let her in, Jade sits down and stares out the window in silence. I wait a minute or so, then make a simple observation.

"You're late," I say in a matter-of-fact kind of way.

"Yup."

"Can you tell me why?"

"I don't know," she says as she exhales loudly. "Shit happens."

"What kind of shit?"

She shakes her head and sighs. "You know what? You therapists ask way too many questions!"

After a pause, I say, "Isn't asking questions part of our job?"

This is followed by a longer pause, after which she looks at me and says, with a sly grin, "You know what my boyfriend says? He says 'therapist' actually stands for 'the rapist'."

I have no idea how to respond to that. My mind starts spinning. I take a few breaths and try to put my confusion into words, "I don't know what that's supposed to mean," I finally say.

She looks away and says, "Well, just like rapists want to get inside your body, therapists want to get inside your mind."

I feel an urge to call my supervisor and ask for advice. But of course, I can't do that. Instead, I remember something she told me in one of our recent sessions: "When in doubt," she said, "don't say anything. Just wait." So I just wait.

Jade finally looks back at me and says, "Aren't you going to say anything?"

"I'm not sure what to say." Then I pause before adding, "And it sounds like you're not sure you want to be here."

"You got that right," she says as she looks away once again.

This wasn't exactly what I signed up for when I decided to become a therapist. I imagined working with clients who were active participants in their treatment, partners in a therapeutic alliance that helps them discover the inner truths that can set them free. Clearly, I had underestimated the power of resistance, a defense most clients use to keep those truths hidden, not only from their therapists, but from themselves.

As I sat there watching Jade stare out the window, wondering what to say next, a thought flashed through my mind: *Gee, maybe I should have stayed in advertising.* But I quickly dismissed it. *No,* I reminded myself, *you left the ad biz because you were tired of sitting around in meetings with people pretending they cared about selling their clients' widgets when all they really cared about was making money and winning awards. You were tired of being one of those people yourself. You wanted to work in a setting where people could just be themselves. Where they could be real. And that's exactly what Jade was doing – and being.*

I also wanted to work in a setting where I could be more real. More alive. Where I could use my mindfulness practice to stay connected with what I was feeling. And then use that information to connect in a more genuine way with my clients, with other people in general, and with the world around me.

So how could I connect with Jade? I didn't have a clue.

Frank, on the other hand, was easy to connect with. His goals were clear and simple. He claimed he had no interest in exploring his inner demons. All he wanted to do was satisfy his parole officer, find a job, get his own apartment, and stay away from drugs. So I helped him find a Narcotics Anonymous group and urged him to go to meetings and connect with a sponsor, which he did. We also talked about triggers, events that made him want to "check out" and use drugs. These included contacts with his old, drug-abusing friends, whom he said he'd stay away from. Plus conflicts with his brother. Since they were living together, these would be more difficult to avoid. His older brother Domenic worked at a big investment firm, and he wasn't happy about having Frank as a long-term house guest. In fact, according to Frank, Domenic seemed ashamed of having a brother who spent time in prison.

"He never lets me forget it," Frank tells me. "But that's no surprise. He always thought he was better than me. And so did my parents."

"What did you think, Frank?"

"I thought he was a tough act to follow. Mr. Straight-and-Narrow. Got good grades, went to college. Now he's a hot-shot financial advisor."

"So you had to find your own way to stand out."

Franks chuckles as he realizes what I'm suggesting, "Yeah, I guess I did, didn't I?"

"And you still can. Without using drugs and without having to go to prison."

As the year went on, Frank got a job as an apprentice carpenter with a small construction company owned by a family friend. His plan was to keep at it and eventually get his union card. He continued going to NA meetings and stayed clean and sober. He also reconnected with an old girlfriend, and by the time my internship at CHA came to an end, the two of them were planning to find a place and move in together.

Things with Jade didn't end so happily. She continued to show up late for our sessions, cancel at the last minute, or just not show up. My supervisor said I needed to tell her that if she continued to miss appointments, I'd have to close her case or arrange a transfer to another therapist. I sent her a letter and left a phone message to that effect, suggesting that a female clinician might be a better fit for her.

When she didn't appear for her next appointment, I checked my voicemail and listened to the message she had just left.

"Yeah, this is Jade, and, um, I got your message, but I can't make it to our appointment today. So you can go ahead and, um, do whatever you have to do to close my case. Anyway, I'm sorry, but I've got a lot going on right now and I just don't have time to be in therapy, OK?"

Then, just before she ended the call, I heard the unmistakable sound of a toilet flushing. Although I was disappointed, I couldn't help but laugh to myself as I put the phone down.

I only wish I was able to save that message so I could listen to it whenever I'm tempted to take myself too seriously.

CHAPTER NINETEEN

Meditation and Psychotherapy Come Together

It's two o'clock in the morning on May 16, 2008, and I can't sleep. Why? Because this is the day I've agreed to give a talk at the third annual Meditation and Psychotherapy Conference sponsored by Harvard Medical School and Cambridge Health Alliance. The conference is taking place in the grand ballroom of the Park Plaza Hotel in Boston and will be attended by over 500 mental health professionals interested in the growing connection between meditation and psychotherapy. And I'm terrified.

I try focusing on my breath and repeating the lovingkindness phrases to myself in an effort to calm down, but nothing seems to help. As I toss and turn, I imagine myself having a panic attack or losing my voice as I step up to the podium to address the crowd. I wonder what the hell I was thinking when I said I'd do this. Finally, I drift off and get a few hours of fitful sleep before the alarm goes off at 6 a.m. I stumble into the shower, put on a suit and tie, and tell Christine, who's attending the conference with me and tends to lose track of time, to please stay focused because I don't want to be late. We get in our car, and I start driving to Alewife Station on the Cambridge/

Arlington line. From there, we'll take the subway into Boston. A few minutes into our drive, probably out of nervousness, I reach up and stroke my chin. But instead of feeling soothed, I'm horrified. For instead of the smooth, freshly shaven skin I expect to find, I discover a bumper crop of day-old stubble.

"Oh, no!" I moan as I glance at Christine. "I forgot to shave!"

She looks at me and says, reassuringly, "Oh, that's OK. Don't worry about it. Nobody's going to notice – or care."

"No, this is terrible. We have to go back."

"Go back? We can't go back!" she says in a more insistent tone. "We'll be late!"

I look at the clock on the dashboard and realize she's right. So instead of turning the car around I keep driving toward my date with destiny. But I'm worried that my slovenly appearance will make me even more self-conscious and less confident than I'm already feeling.

"This is a bad sign," I say, shaking my head in dismay.

"Oh, c'mon," she says, back in reassuring mode. "You're gonna be great."

So how did I end up in such a state of distress? And why was I, a new and unknown practitioner in the world of meditation and psychotherapy, asked to speak to hundreds of professionals at this high-profile conference?

Well, after graduating from social work school in 2001, I was offered a part-time, two-year fellowship in the Program for Psychotherapy at Cambridge Health Alliance, which I gratefully accepted. As a fellow, I could keep seeing the clients I'd been working with as an intern, as well as take on a bunch of new and, if I was lucky, interesting clients. I'd also get regular supervision from three senior clinicians and, along with the other fellows in the program, attend seminars designed to extend our training and help us become better therapists. Plus, I'd get paid for the twenty hours I'd be spending at CHA each week. This was a welcome change after two years of making tuition payments and watching my savings account shrink. It was also a great learning experience.

To round out my schedule, I got a second job working twenty hours a week at the Schiff Center, an adult day treatment program in Cambridge similar to the one at Tri-City Mental Health Center. This was a wonderful opportunity to be part of a treatment team, to feel like part of a community, to build on what I'd learned at Tri-City, and to continue working with clients facing the challenges of severe mental illness.

Two years later, I completed my fellowship at CHA and was asked to stay on as a part-time, fee-for-service clinician. I also passed the state licensing exam and became a Licensed Independent Clinical Social Worker. This meant I could bill insurance companies and open a private practice, which had been my goal since I first started thinking about becoming a therapist. It was a great feeling.

But self-doubt – and my faithful friend Brutus – were still frequent companions. What if I opened a private practice and nobody came? What would I do then? And how could I figure out the logistics of running an office and working with insurance companies? I had no idea.

Fortunately, I made a connection with a local psychologist who helped me get my practice off the ground. Christopher Germer had an office around the corner from mine. Chris was also on the board of the Institute of Meditation and Psychotherapy, a group of therapists whose mission is to bring these two disciplines together. Since I was interested in the same thing, I'd been following IMP for years and admired their work. So I reached out to Chris, told him a little about myself, and asked if we could meet for lunch. He agreed, and he soon became a mentor and friend. Chris advised me to get on as many insurance panels as possible and helped me figure out the best way to do that. He also showed me some of the forms I'd need to meet the legal and professional requirements of a psychotherapist in private practice. Most important, he began sending clients my way.

I also signed up for a monthly supervision group Chris was leading. And the two of us continued to get together every so often for lunch. I began attending lectures and other events sponsored by the Institute for Meditation and Psychotherapy. Then, in 2007, Chris asked me to join the IMP board, and I jumped at the chance. This was an opportunity to meet other like-minded therapists and raise my profile by participating in IMP programs for clinicians who want to learn how to bring meditation and psychotherapy together.

Chris was also one of the two co-directors of the annual Meditation and Psychotherapy conference in Boston. He and Ron Siegel, the other co-director, asked me if I'd like to be one of the speakers at the 2008 edition. Having a deeply rooted and long-standing fear of public speaking, I wanted to say no. But I realized this was a rare opportunity and I'd be foolish to turn it down. So that was how I found myself on the main stage in the grand ballroom of the Park Plaza hotel, preparing to speak to the assembled multitude, feeling nervous and listening to Brutus tell me I didn't deserve to be there. Thankfully, I wasn't one of the featured speakers, who were each given an hour for their talks. That would have been way too much for me to take on. Instead, I was part of a four-person panel. Our topic was "From the Monastery to the Therapy Office: Meditation for Difficult Clinical Relationships," and we each had fifteen minutes to present a relevant case.

So would this be my fifteen minutes of fame – or infamy? I was about to find out.

As Christine and I drove to the conference, I continued to obsess about the unsightly growth on my cheeks and chin. Which might have been a good thing. At least I wasn't worrying about my talk. And by the time we arrived at the Park Plaza, I'd come up with a plan. I knew our four-person panel was scheduled for the final hour of the day. I also knew that my brother-in-law Lawrence had an office in Boston's Back Bay, just a short walk from the conference. I figured I could sneak out during one of the morning talks, pick up a razor and some shaving cream at CVS, run over to Lawrence's office, and make myself more presentable. When I told Christine what I was planning to do, she said I was crazy. But I was not to be deterred. Around mid-morning, I arrived at Lawrence's office, explained the situation, and asked if I could use his bathroom. He just laughed and said, "Go for it!" And when I emerged freshly shaven about five minutes later, I felt ready to take on the world.

For the rest of the day, my mood continued to yo-yo between cautious optimism and abject terror. My inner coach would say, "You got this, pal!" Then Brutus would chime in with, "Who are you kidding? You're gonna bomb!" Finally, the clock struck four and I took a seat on the stage with my three co-panelists. As I listened to the first two speakers, I could feel my mouth getting dry, my throat getting tight, and my breath getting shallow. But I kept breathing and wishing myself well. And when Ron Siegel, our moderator, introduced me I felt surprisingly calm. I had rehearsed my talk so many times, I practically knew it by heart. I had carefully timed it and knew it to be exactly fifteen minutes long. So I stepped up to the podium, took a deep breath, and began telling the audience about my work with Roger, a client with major depression. I described how, for the longest time, he wasn't making progress. In fact, he seemed to be sinking even deeper into hopelessness and despair. Then finally, after much resistance, and a little guidance from me, he used the combination of meditation and psychotherapy to not only recover, but also make some positive changes in his life.

As I told the tale, I glanced at my notes but mostly looked out at the crowd. I also concentrated on speaking directly into the microphone, trusting it to carry my voice to the back of the large hall, and focused on my breath as well as the sound of my voice as a way to stay connected to the aliveness of the present moment. And I actually started to enjoy myself. Everything seemed to be going well until Ron, whose job as moderator included timing the speakers, handed me a slip of paper saying I had just five minutes left. This surprised me, because according to my calculations, I still had about ten minutes worth of material to cover. What had gone wrong? Had I mistimed myself when I practiced at home? Was I speaking more slowly now that I was on the big stage? I didn't know what to think. But instead of protesting or worrying about it, I just skipped over the next section in my notes and went straight to the happy ending. When I finished, the audience responded with warm applause. And at the end of the day, friends and strangers alike told me how much they enjoyed my talk. Best of all, in his closing remarks, Ron confessed to the crowd that he'd been confused about the time and cut me off five minutes before he should have. He also speculated that perhaps it was my mindfulness practice that helped me respond instead of react, to keep going without protesting or missing a beat. This brought a few appreciative laughs from the crowd. And I left the conference feeling not just victorious but vindicated.

My position at the Institute for Meditation and Psychotherapy led to other opportunities, such as hosting a monthly Buddhist psychology lecture series, speaking at smaller conferences, and teaching a class on mindfulness and depression in IMP's year-long certificate course. I was also asked to write a chapter on mindfulness and depression for the second edition of *Mindfulness and Psychotherapy,* a textbook for clinicians. And I co-authored another book for clinicians with my IMP colleagues Susan Pollak and Ron Siegel. We called it *Sitting Together: Essential Skills for Mindfulness-Based Psychotherapy*, and within a few months of its release, the publisher declared it "an instant bestseller."

The publication of these books led to more speaking opportunities, which turned out to be a mixed blessing, because despite my success at the conference in Boston, my aversion to public speaking has remained stubbornly in place. I still get nervous beforehand, even though things usually go well. Another problem is that when I speak to a group about mindfulness and psychotherapy, I'm sometimes left with the uncomfortable feeling that I've become an evangelist and, like the ad man I used to be, that I'm over-hyping this whole mindfulness thing. Is this true? Or is it just another potshot from Brutus? I'm not sure. I firmly believe that meditation has helped me make many changes for the better in my own life, and that it has helped many of my clients do the same. But I also know that it's not a panacea, that it isn't for everyone, and that despite my years of daily practice and my attendance at dozens of retreats, I still have my share of unresolved issues and neurotic suffering.

In other words, the experience of enlightenment – at least the one described by Ram Dass in *Journey to Awakening* – remains an elusive goal.

CHAPTER TWENTY

Roger's Story

By the time I gave that talk at the Harvard Medical School conference, I had a full-time private psychotherapy practice. In addition to my work with individuals, I was also leading Mindfulness Based Cognitive Therapy (MBCT) groups with Dr. Jerome Bass, a psychiatrist and fellow meditator I became friends with many years before at the Cambridge Insight Meditation Center. Jerry was a great source of support and encouragement during the years I couldn't decide whether I really wanted to leave the ad biz and become a therapist.

Sometime in 2006, Jerry read *Mindfulness Based Cognitive Therapy for Depression,* by the Canadian psychologist Zindel Segal and two British colleagues, Mark Williams and John Teasdale. He was excited about it and urged me to get a copy. In the book, the authors describe an 8-week group program they created to help people recover from depression and prevent relapse by using a combination of cognitive therapy and mindfulness meditation. They developed the MBCT program in conjunction with the British government with the goal of reducing the toll depression was taking on the British people and, by extension, the British economy. In randomized controlled studies, MBCT proved to be as effective as antidepressant medication in preventing relapse and more effective in reducing symptoms and improving patients' quality of life. Today, it's offered all over Great Britain by the National Health Service and is available in an increasing number of other countries as well.

How does it work? Each 8-week MBCT group meets once a week for two hours, and in these meetings, participants practice a variety of mindfulness meditation skills. Over the next eight weeks, they also learn cognitive therapy skills they can use to identify and deconstruct their negative thoughts. In addition to the weekly group meetings, participants spend about 45 minutes a day on their homework, which includes daily mindfulness meditation sessions along with some reading and other activities.

In the first edition of their book, Segal, Williams and Teasdale offered handouts and other materials that clinicians could photocopy and use to start MBCT groups in their own communities. The only warning the authors expressed was that before leading their own MBCT groups, clinicians should make sure they've had extensive experience practicing mindfulness meditation themselves, so they'd be able to talk about and teach it as practitioners who know it from the inside out.

Jerry had an inquisitive mind and a generous heart. He was also a low-key guy who loved to kid around and talk about everything from food to national politics to the local sports teams. A native of Philadelphia, he moved to the Boston area for college and medical school. Despite having a stutter, he bravely decided to pursue a career in psychotherapy, the so-called "talking cure." When we first read about MBCT, he had a job prescribing psychiatric medication at a community mental health center and a private practice doing psychotherapy and prescribing medication to his clients. And it was Jerry who decided we should offer the MBCT program to folks in the Boston area.

"W-w-we could do this!" Jerry said to me one day after we both read *Mindfulness Based Cognitive Therapy for Depression*.

"Gee, I don't know, Jerry. Your office isn't big enough for a group, and neither is mine."

"That's no p-p-problem. I'm sure we can find a group room somewhere."

As usual, I had doubts. "What about clients?" I asked. "Where will we find them?"

"We'll just put the w-w-word out there," he said, smiling at me confidently. "I know lots of p-p-people, and so do you. Besides, you're the former ad guy. You can do the m-m-marketing."

I remained skeptical, but Jerry's enthusiasm was infectious. I was also intrigued by his idea. Leading MBCT groups would be an opportunity to do more than just talk about bringing meditation and psychotherapy together. By teaching mindfulness meditation skills within the context of a therapy group, Jerry and I could help people experience the synergistic benefits that can occur when these two disciplines – one Eastern, the other Western – come together.

With Jerry taking the lead, we rented a group room halfway between his office and mine, and we let our friends and colleagues know we were offering this promising new treatment for depression. Soon, the referrals started coming in and we had enough people signed up to launch our first MBCT group.

Among the participants in that first group was Roger, who was one of my individual clients and whose story I told at the Meditation and Psychotherapy conference in Boston. Today, after leading dozens of MBCT groups, I still consider him to be the person who experienced the most dramatic benefits from what he learned in the program.

The first time I saw Roger he was sitting in my waiting room, holding a pair of crutches, wearing sweatpants and an oversized sweatshirt.

He was in his late thirties and had streaks of gray in his dark brown hair, which looked like it hadn't been washed or combed in a while. I showed him into my office and asked why he was seeking psychotherapy.

"My life's a mess," he said as he laid his crutches on the floor, sat back on my sofa, and tried to make himself comfortable. "I'm on a leave of absence from work because I had surgery on my leg about six weeks ago, and it hasn't been healing properly."

"What was the surgery for?" I asked.

"I was in a car accident a few years ago and the leg got smashed up pretty bad. So I've had to go through a bunch of surgeries to repair it. This last operation was supposed to be the final one, but the incision got infected. It still hasn't healed, and I'm still in pain."

"How are you doing mentally and emotionally?"

"Not so good," he said as he looked down at the floor. "I've been feeling down...and discouraged. I started seeing a psychiatrist a while back, and she prescribed an antidepressant. But it hasn't helped. She thought I should start seeing a therapist, too."

"And what do you think?"

"I think it's a good idea," he said. "I don't want to be on medication anyway. Since I started taking it, I've gained 20 pounds, and I feel like a slob."

Roger's injured leg was just part of the problem. He was also divorced and was sharing custody of his young son with his ex-wife. She asked for the divorce after getting involved with another man, which filled Roger with feelings of anger, betrayal, and unworthiness. When the marriage ended, he had several brief, unsatisfying relationships with women he met online, each of which left him feeling more and more hopeless. When I asked what his goals were, he said, "I'd like to be in a committed, long-term relationship, and I'd like to find inner peace. But as far as I can tell, those two things are mutually exclusive."

Roger also told me he'd been reading about Buddhism and meditation, and he wanted to work with a therapist familiar with mindfulness-based approaches, which was why he contacted me.

We agreed to begin meeting weekly. I learned that Roger was raised by an alcoholic single mother who struggled to make ends meet. He never knew his father and never felt loved by his mother, who was preoccupied with her own problems. The injury to his leg and the recent weight gain just added to his sense of being defective and unlovable. But Roger also had strengths. He had always been a good student, and he was especially good at math and science. After college he landed a job with a startup software company. As the company prospered, so did he, and he was in a good position financially. His successful career, along with his commitment to being a good father to his son, were important sources of self-esteem.

When I asked about his interest in meditation, he said he'd read some articles and a book about it, and it made a lot of sense to him, but he hadn't actually tried it. To get him started I taught him a basic mindfulness of breathing exercise. I also suggested we take three minutes at the start of each session to practice this exercise together, and I encouraged him to try practicing for longer periods at home.

The early results were disappointing. Roger said he found it difficult to practice on his own because his mind was "too busy" and "too full of negative thoughts." Like many beginners, he had ideas about what meditation *should* feel like, and he felt discouraged when his practice wasn't living up to those expectations. He also brought his self-critical tendencies to his meditation practice. He'd think, "I just can't do this" or "What's wrong with me?" To help him counteract these negative thought spirals, I told him about lovingkindness practice, but he said he couldn't imagine sending himself such sappy, self-indulgent sentiments. "That's a little too woo-woo for me," he insisted.

Meanwhile, he kept ruminating about his inability to be in a long-term relationship, often experiencing the same kind of negative thinking in this area of his life. "It's no use," he'd say. "Maybe I should just give up."

Through it all, I relied on my own mindfulness practice to help myself bring acceptance and compassion to Roger's situation, as well as to the frustration and helplessness I sometimes felt as I worked with him. I did my best to stay connected with his pain, as well as my own, and to remain hopeful that together, we could find a healthier way for him to relate to his external problems and his inner experience.

So when Jerry and I put together our first MBCT group, I told Roger about it and suggested he try it as a way to deepen his mindfulness practice. He agreed, and it became a turning point in our work together.

Initially, Roger's experience in the group was far from positive. In our individual session a few days after his first MBCT meeting, he told me he was thinking about dropping out of the group because "it just felt weird" and "I kept getting distracted by the woman next to me because her breathing was so loud." I listened and empathized and asked him to stick with it. I also encouraged him to keep up with the homework, which he promised to do. Then, about halfway through the 8-week program, he came to our individual meeting looking, for the first time ever, happy and excited.

"Something clicked this week when I was doing the homework," he said with a smile. "And I think I finally understand what mindfulness is all about."

"Tell me more," I said.

"It's like everything's turned upside down, but in a good way. I feel like I can be aware of all these thoughts and feelings, even the negative ones, without taking them so seriously. Without believing them. I can just watch them come and go. I'm also starting to rethink what I need to be happy. Maybe being in another relationship isn't the answer after all."

Roger seemed more alive than I'd ever seen him before. And by the time he completed the MBCT program, his leg had healed and he'd put his crutches away. He was back to working full time and was committed to his daily meditation practice. He was also taking a class at CIMC, and he even participated in a daylong retreat there. In our individual sessions, Roger was more positive and confident. A transformation had begun. Later, when he said he wanted to go off his antidepressant medication, his psychiatrist and I supported that decision. He joined a gym and lost the weight he'd gained. After a few more months, and after canceling several of our appointments because of schedule conflicts, he said he was ready to stop therapy because he was just too busy with his job, his son, his life. It was time to move on.

That sounded about right to me, and we said good-bye.

About a year later, I got an email from Roger with an update. He said he was still doing well and wanted to thank me for putting him "on a path that has changed (and is still changing) my life." He also said he was still meditating daily and was about to go on a weeklong retreat at the Spirit Rock Meditation Center in California. Then, almost as an afterthought, he said he had met "someone wonderful" who was "very interested in meditation and Buddhism and in growing with me," and that the two of them had decided to get married and build a new life together.

I wish I could say that everyone who completed the MBCT program with Jerry and me experienced the same kind of improvement Roger did. But that would be false advertising. For one thing, very few people who participated in the program were also clients we worked with individually. So I don't really know how they fared, especially after the program was over. However, Jerry and I always asked for feedback during the last meeting of each group, and almost all the participants said they'd benefitted from the program and planned to continue making meditation part of their daily lives. In fact, several participants in one of our early MBCT groups asked me to start a follow-up group to help them stay on track. This Mindfulness Support Group began in the fall of 2010 and met regularly until early 2021. It was extremely gratifying for me to watch the members of this group continue to grow and support each other while using their mindfulness skills to get through periodic bouts of depression and challenging life events, including the COVID-19 pandemic we all experienced together.

At the same time, Jerry and I continued offering the MBCT program twice a year until 2014, when we were suddenly and rudely interrupted.

On a warm night that summer, as we were beginning to interview participants for our fall group, Jerry called and said he'd been experiencing memory loss, confusion, and other neurological symptoms. He wasn't sure what the problem was and said he'd be undergoing a series of tests at a Boston hospital. He wanted me to know because he thought he might not be able to lead the fall MBCT group with me. Of course, I was concerned. But I wasn't prepared for what I heard next. A few weeks later, he told me he'd been diagnosed with Creutzfeldt-Jacob Disease, a rare degenerative brain disorder for which there's no treatment or cure. About 70% of the people who get this disease die within a year. Despite the grim prognosis, Jerry accepted it with equanimity and, at times, a sense of humor. I'll never forget the night Christine and I visited him and his family that summer and brought them a take-out dinner from Wild Willie's, a local burger joint that was one of Jerry's favorite haunts. We ended the evening with Jerry leading all of us in a rousing rendition of, "When You're Happy and You Know it, Clap Your Hands!" For as long as he could, he kept smiling, staying in touch with friends, and continuing to meditate. He died peacefully at home about a month later.

Jerry had been a close friend for almost 25 years and a professional colleague for over ten. His death left a hole in my life similar to the one left by my friend Jim Baker's death sixteen years earlier. But I carried on and led the fall MBCT group that year without him. I continued offering the program twice a year until 2020 when, because of the COVID-19 pandemic as well as the fact that the MBCT program was becoming more widely available in the Boston area, I decided it was time to take a break.

CHAPTER TWENTY-ONE

The End is Near

The untimely deaths of my friends Jim and Jerry reminded me that our days on this earth are numbered.

A similar event occurred in late 2003, just before my fiftieth birthday, when Christine was diagnosed with uterine cancer. We were concerned, of course, but cautiously optimistic. Her surgeon at Massachusetts General Hospital was a rising star, a strong and caring woman who said Christine's cancer was curable, and that after surgery she'd most likely be cancer-free and wouldn't need any further treatment. So after driving the two of us to Boston early on the morning of December 31st – New Year's Eve – and holding Christine's hand as she was wheeled into surgery, I hunkered down in the waiting room, telling myself all would be well. Around noon, when there was still no word from the operating room, I took myself out to lunch at a Thai restaurant and tried to stay positive. When I returned, there was still no news. Finally, a call came down from the OR saying the operation was successful, and the surgeon was on her way to speak with me. At first, I was relieved. But when she walked into the waiting room and our eyes met, I didn't like the look on her face.

"I removed the tumor," she said in a businesslike tone, "but I was surprised to see it had spread beyond the uterus into the endometrium. So I removed a number of lymph nodes from the surrounding area, and I've sent them to the lab to see if the cancer has spread any further. Do you have any questions?"

Yes, I had lots of questions. But I was so taken aback by the news, and by the somber way the doctor – who had been warm and engaging in our previous meetings – delivered it, that I couldn't find the words. So I said, "Right now, just one. When can I see Christine?"

"She's in recovery room, and they'll probably call you in an hour or so to say you can come up and see her."

Then she shook my hand and left.

When I saw Christine, she was groggy from the anesthesia, and happy the surgery was over. She hadn't been told about the cancer spreading and the removal of lymph nodes, and I wasn't about to break the news to her. After she was moved to a room on the surgical floor, I went home and had a restless night of worry and interrupted sleep. The next morning, New Year's Day, I got a call from Christine. Earlier that morning, she had been roused from a blissful, morphine-induced slumber by the resident physician on the floor, who was making the rounds with a group of interns. At 5:30 a.m., he walked into her room, turned on the bright overhead lights, ripped off the bandages covering her incision, said "everything looks good" to his entourage, then proceeded to inform Christine that in addition to the cancerous tumor, the surgeon removed 33 lymph nodes from the surrounding area and sent them to the lab for testing. Startled and confused, she asked this stranger a few basic questions but got no answers except "everything will *probably* be fine." By the time she called me, she was worried about the news and angry about the way it was delivered. When I arrived at the hospital that morning, she was still upset and uncertain about what lay ahead. And that was how 2004, our year of battling cancer, began.

After a series of tests, Christine's diagnosis was changed from stage one uterine cancer to stage three endometrial cancer. The lab determined that at least one of the removed lymph nodes contained fast-dividing cancer cells. This meant it was a dangerous and aggressive form of the disease. A post-surgical PET scan showed that two lymph nodes near her heart were also infected. This was bad news. To stop it from spreading further, one of her doctors, the head of gynecological cancers at MGH at the time, told us, "We're gonna hit this really hard." He said as soon as she recovered from her surgery, she'd begin six rounds of chemotherapy, spaced three weeks apart, followed by six weeks of daily radiation treatments. Then she'd have more scans and tests to see where things stood.

It was a brutal regimen. The chemo drugs were toxic to the max. The medical personnel who administered them had to wear hazmat suits to protect themselves. After the first infusion, Christine lost all her hair in two weeks. So she got a wig, along with some new hats and head scarves. And she remained positive. She even went back to work part time. But by the time the fourth infusion rolled around, the cumulative effects had worn her down. She felt weak and sick, had no appetite, and eating was difficult anyway because of painful sores in her mouth. In related developments, her toenails turned black, and her feet were numb. She said her body felt like a nuclear waste dump, and she didn't think she could take another round. Instead, she took an extended leave of absence from work. Her doctors were split about whether to continue the chemo treatments, but since the blood marker they were tracking – CA-125 – was back in the normal range, they decided to stop. The fact that she said she'd rather die than get more chemo might have influenced their decision. After the chemo, she was given a few weeks to recover before starting the radiation.

Meanwhile, I was struggling to support her while also trying to get my fledgling career as a therapist off the ground. I was still working at Cambridge Health Alliance and the Schiff Center, and I had just opened my private practice. Suddenly, I was also doing a lot of cooking, cleaning, running errands, and going to medical appointments. So I was tired. I was also worried about where all this was heading. Watching Christine go from a strong, healthy woman to a bald, weakened, partially disabled cancer patient in just a few weeks broke my heart. And it filled me with dread about what the future might bring.

Once she started the daily radiation, things let up for a while. She felt fine for the first two weeks and was able to work part-time once again. But as the days went by, the effects of the radiation took a toll. One day, while seeing a client, she had to run to the bathroom because of a sudden diarrhea attack. And this was just a sign of things to come. Since her lower abdomen was getting zapped, her digestive system was bearing the brunt of the daily doses of radiation. I'll refrain from providing details but suffice it to say that by the end of the six weeks, she had lost 10% of her body weight and was in rough shape.

She had begun cancer treatment in January and was finally done – or at least we hoped she was – in July. She was incredibly brave and positive throughout, and I did my best to help. Our network of friends and family also stepped up to bring us food, take Christine to her appointments, and offer emotional support, for which we were very thankful. Throughout that summer and early fall, her post-treatment blood tests looked good. Her hair grew back, and she regained some of the weight she lost. We remained grateful to her doctors and the other professionals who helped her make it through the months of treatment. And we actually started to believe she'd won a long, difficult battle. But we knew the next few months would be crucial. The doctor who headed her team warned us: "Now is the hard part," he said. "In about a third of the women with this kind of cancer, it comes back. And if it does come back, it usually comes back fast."

About a week before Thanksgiving, there was bad news. Her CA-125 count had shot up. To rule out a fluke, the test was repeated, and the count was still high. We weren't sure what this meant, so we scheduled an appointment with the chief oncologist. Despite his lofty status, he was a kind man, and had always been available to answer Christine's questions and concerns. Once, he even responded to an anxious email she sent in the middle of the night, and his quick answer eased her fears and helped her go back to sleep.

As I drove the two of us to the hospital, I did my best to feel my breath, stay in my body, and stay in the present moment. Christine was sitting beside me, humming along with a song on the radio. We didn't talk much as we looked for a spot in one of the MGH parking garages, made our way to the cancer center and checked in. We had to wait about twenty minutes before we could see the doctor, which was typical, and during that time, my anxiety spiked. Every so often, I'd look over at Christine and smile, and she'd smile back. She'd done a lot of thinking about this and had told me she was ready to hear the news, whatever it was.

Finally, we were called into the doctor's office. He was a big man with a full head of gray hair, and he was wearing the traditional white coat. He had an authoritative but not intimidating presence. We recently learned that his wife was undergoing treatment for breast cancer, which made us feel closer to him. He greeted us warmly and asked us to sit down while he took a seat behind his desk and pulled out Christine's file.

After a few preliminaries, Christine asked the first question.

"So my CA-125 count went up," she said. "What exactly does that mean?"

He sighed, looked at her and said, "I'm sorry, but it probably means your cancer is back."

"And what does 'probably' mean?" I asked.

He took a moment, glanced up at the ceiling, perhaps for guidance, and said, "Well, I suppose the elevated CA-125 could be caused by an unrelated infection, but given the timing, I'd say there's about a 95% chance the cancer is back."

Then I asked, "And if it's back, what do we do?"

"If it came back this quickly, I'm afraid there's nothing more we can do," he said as he looked at Christine. "The amount of radiation you received was the equivalent of being exposed to a small atomic bomb. Your body wouldn't be able to handle more treatment."

Without hesitation, Christine said, "I wouldn't want to go through that again anyway. But I don't think it's back. And if it is, then just make me comfortable."

This apparent death sentence brought our conversation to a painful stop. The doctor finally broke the silence by reminding us that we still didn't know for sure. To find out, he said she could either schedule a PET scan now, which would be more conclusive, or she could come back for another blood test after the holidays to check her CA-125 count. If it was back to normal, it would mean the spike was caused by something else. But if it was still high, which he had said was 95% likely, it would mean the cancer was back.

Not wanting to put herself through another PET scan, Christine decided to come back for more blood work after the holidays.

For both of us, though for different reasons, the next six weeks were surreal, dream-like, and at times, nightmarish. We'd been told there was a high likelihood her cancer had returned and would soon lead to her death. We shared this sad news with a few close friends, but we didn't tell our families because it was the holiday season and we didn't want to spoil it for them, especially if the 5% chance it was a false alarm turned out to be true. So we celebrated Thanksgiving and Christmas, and every night, we held each other close. I felt her breathing as she slept, and if I couldn't sleep, I'd lie there and meditate, focusing on the feeling of my breath as it flowed in and out, synchronizing it at times with hers, reminding myself that in this moment we're both alive and warm, that the future is unknown, and that right now we're both breathing and we're both well. And that's just the way things are. In fact, that's almost always the way things are. We never know for sure when death will take us. Eventually, I'd drift off to sleep, too. In many ways, I've never felt so close to Christine, and so alive myself, as I did during those weeks of uncertainty.

It was a time when I understood in a deeper way that being fully present and alive in each moment is the best we can do, the best we can hope for – and what life is really all about.

It was an important time for Christine, too. She thought a lot about death, and she told me she'd reached the point where, whether the cancer was back or not, she'd be fine either way.

"That's good to know, hon," I said. "I'm glad you feel that way. But I'm not there yet. And I'm not letting myself think about it too much. Not yet anyway. Not until we get the results of the next blood test."

It was a long six weeks, to say the least. She finally had her blood drawn in early January, but we didn't get the results for several stressful days. On one of those days, I drove her to an acupuncture appointment. She'd started receiving acupuncture treatments almost a year earlier to alleviate the side effects of the chemo and radiation, and I sometimes got a treatment myself to help manage my anxiety and insomnia. But that day, I was just the driver. After the appointment, we were in the lobby putting our coats on when Christine's phone rang. It was her surgeon. All I heard was this:

"Hello. Yes, this is Christine." (LONG PAUSE) "Oh, that's great! That's wonderful!! Yes, thank you! Thank you so much for calling!!!"

Then she hung up, looked at me, smiled and said, "I'm OK. My CA-125 is back to normal!"

We hugged each other and started jumping up and down, like a pitcher and a catcher who just recorded the final out in game seven of the World Series, or two kids who just learned they were going to Disney World, or two strangers in Times Square who just got the news that World War II was finally over. It was a moment of unmitigated joy and unexpected relief. We had somehow beaten the odds. It felt like a miracle. When we got home, a friend who knew we were waiting to hear from the doctor called me. As I tried to tell him the good news, I choked up and couldn't get the words out. So I handed the phone to Christine, who filled him in.

For the next few weeks, we were simply happy to be alive. But after the initial rush of giddiness and gratitude wore off, we found ourselves settling into a new and unfamiliar normal. Christine went back to work at Cambridge Health Alliance, while I kept working in the outpatient clinic at CHA while building my private practice. But things had changed. For Christine, the most obvious changes were physical. She was more easily fatigued. The chemo and radiation caused permanent damage to her digestive system, so she was forced to make changes in her diet. The internal radiation she received through her vagina caused similar damage "down there," and to this day, she continues to experience tenderness and frequent bleeding in that part of her body. As a result, our sex life would never be the same. We also became more aware that our bodies were aging, that we were at a point where we could no longer deny we were in the second half of our lives, and that death had become a more tangible presence.

All this can eventually be liberating, but before that, it can be depressing. After we got the good news that Christine's cancer was gone, she continued to recover and feel better, but I sank into a low-grade depression. My symptoms were difficulty sleeping, a lack of pleasure in things I normally find pleasurable, and a tendency to ruminate about past "mistakes." In the wee hours before dawn I'd lie in bed, wide awake, thinking things like, *If only I had pushed Christine to seek treatment sooner the cancer would have been detected at an earlier stage and she wouldn't have had to go through all that chemo and radiation and we'd both be much better off now.* Or, *What if she has a recurrence and we need to go through it all again?* Stuff like that. I knew it was crazy, and my mindfulness practice helped me keep it in perspective to a certain extent, but as it persisted, I began to think that maybe I needed help. I didn't want to go back into therapy because it felt more physiological than psychological, so I thought I'd try medication instead. I knew that psychotropic medications were helping many of my clients. And I was curious about what they could do for me. So I met with a psychiatrist and started taking an antidepressant he thought would be helpful. And it did help, especially with sleep. But it also came with a side effect I didn't like at all. About a half hour after taking the pill, I'd experience akathisia, an intense restlessness and jitteriness that made me want to jump out of my skin. This would last for about an hour, then it would pass, and I'd feel relaxed and sleepy. This was troubling to me, and the doctor didn't know what to make of it. So I took the medication for a few months because it did help with sleep, but then, as things settled down for Christine and me, and with my doctor's approval, I stopped.

A few years later, new challenges came into our lives, most of them related to the decline of our elderly parents. In 2011, Christine's mother had heart surgery from which she never recovered. Instead, she spent three months on a ventilator and feeding tube in the ICU of a Long Island hospital before being transferred to a nursing home, where she died a week later. During those months, Christine and I made frequent trips to New York to be with her mother and support her father. He had a number of medical problems of his own, including signs of dementia. After his wife died, he was having trouble functioning, so we took him on a tour of a highly rated assisted living facility in Cambridge, and we urged him to move in so he could get the help he needed and live close to us. When he said he "wasn't ready," we hired one of his New York neighbors to assist him with medications, meals, and household tasks. But we remained concerned, especially about his driving, which he refused to give up. Then, in late 2013, he hit a young woman who was crossing the street in front of his minivan and caused serious injuries that nearly killed her and left her with permanent brain damage. After that, he agreed to stop driving, and in early 2014 he put his house on the market and moved into the assisted living facility we had shown him just a few months earlier.

Meanwhile, my parents were both in their eighties and also struggling with health issues. My father had three terminal illnesses: pulmonary fibrosis, congestive heart failure, and kidney disease. He was weak and had several nasty falls at home. On several occasions, when he couldn't get back up, he had to call my brother Pete, who lived nearby, to come to his rescue. But despite his physical decline, his mind was still sound. On the other hand, my mother was in good shape physically but had lost most of her ability to function in the world due to Alzheimer's disease. Wanting to intervene before a tragedy happened, my sister and I toured the local assisted living facilities and found a place we thought would be the best choice for them. We took them there for lunch and a tour one day, and though they said they liked it, they claimed they "weren't ready." My father was especially reluctant to leave his home in Chelmsford, where he always imagined his wife would take care of him until he died. But since she wasn't able to do that, and since he was having trouble taking care of her as well as himself, my siblings and I convinced him it wasn't safe for them to remain there. Feeling defeated, he begrudgingly agreed to give the assisted living place a try. We were surprised and relieved when he told us shortly after they moved in that "this is the best thing we've ever done." So the two of them were happy there, and we visited them regularly. But their health continued to decline. After a year in assisted living, my father died of respiratory failure in March of 2014. While he was in the process of dying, my mother fell, broke her hip, and was transferred to a nursing home, where she died in December of 2014 from complications of Alzheimer's disease.

During a nine-month span of that year, I lost both parents and two of my closest friends. Jerry Bass, my Dharma buddy and MBCT group co-leader, died of Creutzfeldt Jacob Disease in August. In September, it was Scott Curtis, a fellow Samaritans volunteer I met in 1989 and who remained a close friend. Although he struggled with bipolar disorder, Scott was a poet, a sensitive soul and, like me, a lifelong fan of the Boston Red Sox and the New England Patriots. We had a brief phone conversation one night that September, and he told me he hadn't been feeling well. I didn't realize it at the time, but I'm almost certain I was the last person to speak with him. A few days later, I learned he died in his sleep that same night of a heart attack.

It was a helluva year, and I was glad when it was over. With so much happening at once, however, I didn't have time to absorb and grieve each loss. Instead, I moved from one to the next, then threw myself into my work and didn't look back. This might have been an effective short-term strategy, but things finally caught up with me in early 2016, when I started to feel depressed again. This became clear to me at the annual "Vision Meeting" of the Institute for Meditation and Psychotherapy's board of directors, an all-day event where we discuss plans for the year ahead: educational programs we want to offer, books we want to write, movies we want to include in the Buddhist psychology film series, speakers we want to invite to the Buddhist psychology lecture series, ways to make the organization more inclusive and get members more involved. I didn't want to go to the meeting in the first place, and as the day dragged on, I realized I had no interest in any of it. This was hard for me to admit. I also realized that "markedly diminished interest in activities" is a common symptom of depression according to the DSM-V, the manual clinicians use to diagnose mental health disorders.

When the meeting was over, I went home and knew that once again, it was time to seek help. I thought about going back on medication, but I remembered something the psychiatrist said when I decided to go off the medication he had prescribed a number of years before. He reminded me of something I learned during my training as a social worker and that I often told my clients: Medication and psychotherapy can each be effective on their own, but they're usually even more effective when used together. So before I scheduled an appointment with the psychiatrist, I looked for a therapist, which was a humbling experience. I hadn't been in therapy in almost twenty years, and I liked to think I had "graduated," especially now that I was a therapist myself. But I knew those thoughts were coming from a false sense of pride. I also knew that many therapists, including some of my closest colleagues, believe it's important to continue working on their own "stuff" with their own therapists, and I admired them for being willing to do that.

One of my colleagues recommended Daniel, a social worker and psychotherapist with an office nearby. Daniel was a little older than me, and he knew what it was like to lose loved ones and feel the physical and psychological effects of aging. Together, we explored my feelings about some of the recent losses and other changes in my life. He also told me he thought it might be a good idea to go back on medication. So I met with the psychiatrist and asked if we could try a different antidepressant, one that would help with sleep and the persistent negative thinking but without the side effects that came with the medication I took before. He agreed and prescribed a drug that had been helpful to my father during the final two years of his life. It was helpful to me, too, and the only side effect – some minor gastrointestinal distress – was minimal and manageable.

After working with Daniel for a year, I was in a better place. I did some grieving, but I also learned that grief is a process that never completely ends, especially as we get older. I also stepped down from the board and faculty of the Institute for Meditation and Psychotherapy because I wanted to give myself a break and give someone else a chance, which felt like a good decision. Then I thanked Daniel and said goodbye. And a few months later, after talking it over with my psychiatrist, I discontinued the antidepressant once again.

Things went relatively smoothly for the next couple of years. But in 2019, my mood began to sink once more. There were a number of reasons for this unwelcome dip. Christine had retired a year earlier and was enjoying her life of leisure. She was sleeping in whenever she felt like it. She was also taking classes, making art, writing poetry, singing in a chorus, gardening, and taking long walks with our dog. Part of me wanted to join her. But another part was afraid. We were both in our late sixties, and I wasn't sure we'd have enough money to keep living in relative comfort, especially if we both lived to a ripe old age and needed to move into an assisted living place like our parents did. I also felt a responsibility to my clients and didn't want to abandon them with much work still left to be done. To top it off, I wasn't sure what I'd do with all that free time. But the idea of doing something creative, like writing, appealed to me.

Soon, the familiar pattern of indecision, rumination, and insomnia reared its ugly head. Once again, I didn't know what I wanted to do with my life. Should I keep working or retire? In many ways, it was the same feeling I had when I graduated from college and started looking for work. But I was older and wiser now, so instead of continuing to struggle, I went back into therapy. Since Daniel was no longer available, I decided to look for a female therapist. This seemed like a good idea, mostly because I hadn't worked with one since the debacle with Roxanne and New Beginnings forty years earlier. Getting a woman's perspective would be refreshing, I thought, and might also help heal some of the lingering resentment from that unfortunate episode. I scheduled initial meetings with two female clinicians, chose the one who felt like the better fit for me, and became a therapy patient once more. Carla and I hit it off from the start, and she agreed that I should also contact my psychiatrist and go back on the medication if I wanted to, which I did.

Soon after we started working together, the COVID-19 pandemic struck, which complicated matters in many ways, but in other ways made things simpler. A lot of unnecessary activities, like commuting to and from my office, suddenly fell away. I began seeing my clients via telehealth from home and could continue my work with Carla the same way. During our first few sessions, I did a life review, telling her about my search for meaningful work and a loving, long-term relationship, with all the missteps and detours along the way. By sharing my stories, and with Carla's help, I was able to see that I could choose how to describe them, how to make meaning of them, how to hold them in my heart. For example, one story I often told myself, especially when I was depressed, was the one about how I should have stayed with Anita, my college girlfriend. If only I'd done that, the story goes, I'd be happier, more fulfilled, and better off today. But is that true? Of course, there's no way to know for sure. But looking at it realistically, I can say with 100% certainty that I still had a lot of growing up to do back then, that I had no idea what I wanted to do with my life, and that because of my emotional immaturity and lack of direction, if I had stayed with Anita, it's extremely unlikely we would have lived happily ever after. I also realized that telling myself I'd blown my one chance for true happiness was making it difficult for me to find happiness in the here and now.

By letting go of what might have been, I could also better appreciate all the good things that actually exist in my life: a loving relationship with a wonderful partner, supportive friends and family, reasonably good health, a successful first career that helped me accumulate some savings, and a second career that was rewarding in other important ways.

After confronting the past and appreciating the present, I was ready to look to the future. And what I could see quite clearly was that I wanted to slow down. Although I'd stopped accepting new clients a year earlier, I still had a full schedule. But after 18 years of schooling and 46 years of work as a high school teacher, college textbook sales rep, advertising copywriter, and mindfulness-based psychotherapist, I was ready to do as Thoreau had done, to retreat to my own version of the Concord woods "because I wished to live deliberately, to front only the essential facts of life, and see if I could learn what it had to teach, and not, when I came to die, discover that I had not lived."

Toward the end of 2020, I set my retirement date for May 1, 2021. And I started the process of telling my clients that I'd spend the next few months wrapping things up with them and, if they wished, helping them find new therapists.

I also started writing the first draft of this memoir.

CHAPTER TWENTY-TWO

Amazing Grace

As I begin this final chapter and as I look back on my life, I find myself wanting to address three important questions:

1. Did I find my true calling?
2. Did I find true love?
3. Was it worth all the effort?

And as far as I can tell, the three answers are:

1. That's not a fair question.
2. Neither is that.
3. Yes.

I believe only a few rare individuals in this world can claim to have a true calling. Like those prodigies who, from a tender young age, show an amazing ability to play the piano, solve complex math problems, or shoot a basketball – and then go on to become concert pianists, groundbreaking astrophysicists, or NBA champions. Or, as a less spectacular example, there's someone like my cousin Jim, who always knew he wanted to be a doctor, went on to become one, and never looked back.

For most of us, thinking in terms of "true calling" is probably a mistake. It's the kind of idealism that just sets us up for a major letdown in the real world. If we're lucky, we have a rough idea of what we'd like to do for a living, and we find something that at least comes close to what we think we want. If we're not so lucky, we settle for whatever comes along and hope for the best.

My quest was complicated by the fact that I was someone who always kept his eye on the audience. Since I was so concerned about what *they* wanted, I had a hard time figuring out who I was and what I wanted. This was especially true during childhood and adolescence, when the path my parents and teachers expected me to follow was clear. All I had to do was keep putting one foot in front of the other. But everything changed when I graduated from college and found myself at a crossroads with no signposts to guide me. Although my parents declined to weigh in, I knew they hoped I'd do something that would lead to a conventional definition of success, something that would make me rich and/or famous, something they could brag about to their friends. But I wanted to find a career that would be both meaningful and creative. So in a minor act of rebellion and self-determination, I decided to become a high school English teacher, a decision that didn't work out so well. When I eventually made my way into the advertising business, I found something that represented a compromise. It provided enough material success to satisfy my family's aspirations for me, and it gave me a chance to do something creative.

As an unexpected bonus, I was lucky enough to stumble upon something I was good at. I happened to have a knack for writing catchy headlines and coming up with ideas that sell. And it was fun, at least for a while. But it didn't sustain me. I mean, just because you're good at something doesn't mean you should keep doing it, right? What if you're good at picking people's pockets? Should you try building a career around that specialized skill? Probably not. So after laboring in the advertising trenches for 23 years, I finally decided to do something that was more in line with my values – and more meaningful than stringing a bunch of clever words together or winning an award for creativity.

For the next 23 years, I was a clinical social worker and psychotherapist. And I've never regretted it. It allowed me to work with others on a deeper, more genuine level. It gave me the opportunity to help all kinds of people figure out how to find happiness in their work lives as well as their personal lives. How to make the most of their strengths and accept their limitations. How to come to terms with the past, live in the present, and build a better future. It was challenging work, and it was frustrating at times, but it was almost always rewarding.

As for "true love," I don't even know what that's supposed to mean. Like "true calling," it suggests an unrealistic ideal that sets us up for disappointment. When I was just 18 years old, I found a love that was passionate and all-consuming, a love that filled me with joy and wonder, a love that burned bright and hot, a love that felt true. But it was a love that didn't last.

When that love ended, I went through a series of relationships that were less than satisfying either for me, my partner, or both of us. Then I met Christine, and I found a love that was not only mutual, but also deeper and more mature than anything I'd experienced before. Yes, there was physical attraction, but the two of us were also drawn to each other because of shared values and interests. As our relationship deepened, I learned something I'd read about but never quite understood: That love is more than a feeling. It's a verb. It's something you do. That the feeling of love needs to be backed up by actions and commitments. So maybe that's what true love is all about. At least that's what I've come to believe.

So if I'm not sure if I found true love or my true calling, how can I say that my years of searching have been worth all the trouble? It's because what I *have* found: the Noble Eightfold Path that was laid out by the Buddha over 2500 years ago. This path has helped me grow, feel more alive, and connect with people in more genuine ways than I ever could before.

It's also because I believe, as Pema Chodron says in her book *When Things Fall Apart,* that "the path is the goal."

In other words, there's no map to follow and no final destination. The path is continuously arising and passing away in each moment. Our job is to surrender to it and see where it takes us. It's the path Jack Kornfield has called "a path with heart." A path that includes our work and our relationships with one another but goes far beyond these temporary manifestations that appear in our lives. It's a path that leads to a deeper understanding of who we are and how we're all interconnected. A path that ultimately allows us to see through the illusions of the material world into the true nature of reality. Buddhists call this *nirvana* or enlightenment. Other religions call it salvation, oneness, union with the divine, eternal life, and many other things. Words cannot describe it. But even if we can't describe or attain it, we can approach it by walking on a path with heart.

I've taken many detours in my life, but through my work in psychotherapy, my relationship with Christine, and my practice on the meditation cushion, I've always been able to find my way back to this path with heart. Not that I've done it all by myself. All along, I believe I've been helped by a force I don't fully understand. Dylan Thomas called it "the force that through the green fuse drives the flower." It's the force that makes the great earth spin, that pushes the rivers toward the sea and the spermatozoa toward the ovum, that fuels both the expansion and contraction of the universe. The world's great religions have many names for this force, such as the Dharma, the Tao,

The Holy Spirit, The Great Spirit, All That Is, God, Allah, Yahweh, and the one I like best: Grace. Amazing grace.

> *Amazing grace, how sweet the sound*
> *That saved a wretch like me.*
> *I once was lost, but now I'm found;*
> *Was blind but now I see.*

It was grace that led me to that life-altering conversation with Lotte Steinfeld in Wilmette, Illinois. To those formative jobs as an aspiring copywriter with mentors like Brian Turley and Terry MacDonald. To the offices of therapists like Jonathan, Richard, Daniel, and Carla. To that spiritual bookstore on Fifth Avenue and my encounter with the teachings of Ram Dass. To that first meditation retreat with Larry Rosenberg at the Insight Meditation Society. To subsequent retreats with Joseph Goldstein, Sharon Salzberg, Jack Kornfield and many others, including the one where I met Christine Aquilino, who became my partner for life. It was grace that inspired me to do volunteer work with the Samaritans and two different hospice organizations. That gave me the courage to go back to school and become a psychotherapist. That told me to reach out to Chris Germer, another mentor who helped me build a new career that combined my interests in meditation and psychotherapy.

Of course, I realize I've also enjoyed many advantages that made my journey easier than it otherwise would have been. I grew up in a safe and secure home, with two loving parents who, despite their shortcomings, instilled in me and my three siblings the value of education, discipline, honesty, and hard work. All of which helped us find our places in the world. As a white, cisgender, heterosexual, able-bodied male in the world's richest and most powerful nation, I also grew up with access to privileges that were mostly invisible to me at the time, and that have helped me immeasurably. I went to a prestigious college that was an exclusive white-male enclave for most of its four-hundred-year history. Then I went to work in the advertising business, which also was traditionally dominated by white men. All of this, thank goodness, has been changing. But there's no doubt that the income I earned while I was in advertising enabled me to live a privileged life and accumulate the savings that made my career transition a lot easier than it otherwise would have been. This transition, in turn, allowed me to give something – hopefully, something of value – back to the world.

When I started working on this book, a friend asked me why I felt moved to write it. At the time, I didn't have much of an answer. But now that it's done, I can say that the main reason was a need to tell my story and discover that if in the telling, I could make some sense of it and gain a deeper understanding of the restlessness that drove me from job to job, relationship to relationship, career to career. As I look back now, I can see that this restlessness was actually a healthy impulse. It prevented me from settling for mere material comfort when my heart yearned for something more. It kept me looking for that path with heart.

Another reason for writing the book was the hope that, by sharing my story, I might inspire others to look within themselves and summon the courage to find what they truly want and need in their lives, regardless of their circumstances, instead of seeking the permission or approval of their families, their friends, or the societies in which they live. For you, dear reader, this might mean looking for a new job, going back to school, leaving an unhappy marriage, moving to a different part of the country or another part of the world, exploring a different religion or spiritual path, or even pursuing an outside interest you've always told yourself you don't have time for or wouldn't be any good at. It's what Joseph Campbell meant when he famously exhorted his readers to "follow your bliss."

As for me, the path continues to unfold. Where it goes from here, I cannot say. All I can say for sure is one day I will die, and until I do, I'll do my best to be as fully alive as possible. I'll continue walking on a path with heart for as long as I'm able. At this point in my life, I believe that walking on this path is not so much a search for happiness as it is a search for meaning, understanding, compassion, love, wisdom, and that sense of aliveness we can only experience when we embrace the present moment with awareness and acceptance. Of course, in a universe that's constantly changing in seemingly random ways, finding the ultimate meaning of it all will remain an elusive goal for most of us. But I also believe there's something profoundly important in the search itself.

ACKNOWLEDGMENTS

First and foremost, I'd like to thank my wife and companion on the path, Christine Aquilino, who not only provided helpful comments on my manuscript, but also showed incredible patience and offered unflagging support as I spent countless hours doing everything that had to be done to turn it into a book.

I'd also like to thank the meditation teachers who showed me some extraordinary ways to see the world and myself more clearly, whether it was in person or through their writing, especially Larry Rosenberg, Joseph Goldstein, Sharon Salzberg, Jack Kornfield, Tara Brach, Narayan Helen Liebenson, Michael Grady, Michele McDonald, Pema Chodron, Thich Nhat Hanh, and Ram Dass. The same goes for the therapists who helped me explore other ways to understand my inner world. Although I don't name them here, I trust they know who they are.

My colleagues at the Institute for Meditation and Psychotherapy – especially Chris Germer, Ron Siegel, Susan Pollak, and Paul Fulton – gave me important opportunities to grow professionally and find my voice as both a therapist and a writer.

I'm also grateful to my clients, who had the courage to share their stories with me, some of which appear in this book.

I learned much about the craft of memoir from Judah Leblang, my teacher at Grub Street, who edited the first draft of my manuscript, and from Dorian Fox, who taught a yearlong memoir course at Pioneer Valley Writers Workshop. My classmates at Pioneer Valley also gave me valuable feedback and pushed me to explore material I was reluctant to write about. And a class on the three-act structure taught by Courtney Maum through Domestika enabled me to shape my material into a story.

A number of friends – including Kathy Kiley, Peter Connolly, Al Gentle, Linda Kramer, Paul Goldmuntz, and Colette Bourassa – read drafts of my manuscript at various stages and offered insightful comments.

Lisa Mullenneaux, my editor, helped me in get the manuscript into its final form. And Meradith K., along with her colleagues at Troy Book Makers, did a beautiful job turning it into a book.

Finally, to my parents, Peter and Marianne Pedulla, who both died in 2014, and to my three siblings – Paul Pedulla, Pete Pedulla, and Maryellen McDonnell – I owe a great debt. Their stories are inextricably intertwined with mine – and always will be.

ABOUT THE AUTHOR

After spending 23 years as an award-winning copywriter and creative director in the advertising business, Thomas Pedulla went back to school, got a Master's in Social Work, and spent the next 23 years as a psychotherapist working at the interface between Buddhist meditation and Western psychology. Tom is a co-author of *Sitting Together: Essential Skills for Mindfulness Based Psychotherapy* and a contributing author of *Mindfulness and Psychotherapy, Second Edition,* both published by The Guilford Press. He lives in Massachusetts with his wife, Christine Aquilino, and their dog Luca.